iSpeak Cloud™
Crossing the Cloud Chasm

Jeanne Morain

iSpeak Cloud: Crossing the Cloud Chasm
First print edition, July 2014
ISBN: 978-0-9846757-2-2

August 2014 – First Kindle Edition
ISBN: 978-0-9846757-3-9

Visit us on the web: www.client4cloud.com

Credits

Technical Publication Specialist: Shinji Yaguma
Graphic Design and Artwork: Paul Daniels
Producers: Sheila Mangione & Jeanne Morain
Asst. Producers: Susan Hayward, Cody Morain, Bryce Morain Daniels
Editor: Mangione, Payne & Associates

Dedication

This series is dedicated to the men and women at the companies I have worked for and the clients I have worked with. These people burned the midnight oil to identify and resolve gaps across people, process and technology over the last two decades. In working together, we forged new ground from the client to the cloud.

And to my family (Paul, Cody, Bryce, Emma, Gabriella, The Eubanks-Morain Clan, Mamasan, Yaguma family) and friends for their love, support and sacrifices made not only during the time I have periodically taken off researching and writing books but for all the years spent on the road at customer sites, conferences or in the office. Without all of you, I would not be the person I am today.

Real Heroes

We want to extend a special thank you to everyone who took the time to interview and/or provide feedback for this book. (Many are listed below. However, there are several who couldn't include their names that are also acknowledged for their contribution.)

Lenin Aboagye	Marc Jorgenson
Kamal Ahwalia	Ashish Kharuna
Chris Armstrong	Tom Klemzak
Bryan Ard	Christian Lewis
Alex Barreto	Gabe Maentz
Matt Bausch	Andi Mann
Charlie Betz	Michael Mattal
Chris Cason	Kurt Milne
Brian Cinque	Muneer Mubashir
Bryan Diehl	Suneet Nandwani
Ben Gordon	Paul Peissner
Shane Gunn	Vincent Betancourt
Susan Hayer	James Burdick
Daisy Itty	Paul "Doc" Burnham

Testimonials

In iSpeak Cloud, Jeanne takes the reader through a realist journey most companies face when moving to the "cloud". In this book, as in her other books, Jeanne takes what has proven to be a complicated subject and presented it in a manner that enables readers to grasp the concepts more easily. Her approach of presenting this in a workshop format only strengthens the reader's ability to relate this journey to their experiences as well as provide a useful roadmap. Throughout this book, Jeanne highlights key concepts that are often taken for fact but are usually miss-understood.

– *Paul "Doc" Burnham*, IAITAM Fellow, Technical Consultant

In the technology industry it is a rare occurrence to find the cross-discipline expertise that enjoys the subtle and technical challenges of complex enterprise software, has enough experience to quickly decide on a best next step in difficult situations and the sense of the business needs that need to be addressed. Jeanne Morain is one of those rare talents that is an inspiring realist, a practical visionary and unafraid to take on the status quo and the destructive legacy strangle holds to impair organizations.

I am amazed at her depth and breadth of her technical skills and knowledge, the diversity of her cross-discipline IT experiences over the 2 decades, and the network of industry leaders that she regularly engages with. Jeanne is a lot of fun to watching her work. Her insight, advice and her concerns are always important to listen to.

– *Paul Piessner*, DevOps Evangelists

Thought provoking book provides the recipe to enable IT to explore not only the challenges but best practice solutions for implementing a cohesive Cloud strategy. The dialog style and icons make it easy to imagine yourself participating in the work shop and to understand what it would take to be successful along your Cloud journey. A highly recommended must read for any professional on business or technology looking to incorporate best practices based on hands on experience.

– *Matt Bausch*, Cloud Service Architect

About the Author

Jeanne Morain is the principal researcher and consulting strategist at iSpeak Cloud. She has held various executive roles in marketing, strategic alliances and product management with Flexera Software, VMware and BMC Software (Marimba).

Jeanne has more than 18 years of experience in systems management, virtualization and cloud computing, implementing solutions for millions of users across Fortune 2000 companies for enterprises and independent software vendors. She has won numerous awards for her work in the areas of business service management (BSM), software as a service (SaaS), dynamic data center and virtualization, and is a contributing author and coauthor of books on BSM, virtualization and cloud computing.

Jeanne is best known for her customer-/partner-centric approach to research and solutions. She is a noted industry speaker at VMworld, Interop, CloudSlam, IAITAM, user conferences and SoftSummit. She has written blogs as well as articles for trade publications. Jeanne holds a Master's degree from Southern Illinois University and certification in IT Infrastructure Library. www.ispeakcloud.com, twitter@ JeanneMorain

Foreword

Cloud is the new and ubiquitous term known to both IT and the business. The question is how does one implement cloud without a clear understanding of what it is, what it can offer and the risks versus benefits? Any number of technology firms will help you cloud enable your business. However *iSpeak Cloud* offers a direct view into how a cloud solution should be deployed within a common organization, including members who are new to cloud and those who are not.

iSpeak Cloud allows a reader of nearly any background to jump into the cloud conversation. It encompasses the perspectives of many roles within an organization, all the way from leadership in operation and finance to external consultants and individual contributors. The simple, progressive discussion flow allows you to understand what conversions should occur, when and why, from all the necessary perspectives. The knowledge is presented in dialog format allowing for easy digestion with a high level of understanding and retention.

This book is unique in structure and organization. It offers easy readability while providing valuable information from expert sources. The principal resource in this case is Jeanne Morain, a known expert in the configuration space. Jeanne's background and experience in multiple areas enable her to write from the perspectives of many different organizational roles. The real value exists in the wisdom Jeanne has written into this book. This wisdom is rare, I believe sourced from extensive knowledge in addition to experience of years executing complex implementations.

iSpeak Cloud provides a broad audience with the understanding required for beneficial participation in enterprise cloud deployments. This book is filled with practical real-world advice for the next generation of IT projects.

Chris Armstrong
Enterprise Architect
Teknow Consulting Solutions

Thoughts for Your Cloud Journey

Jeanne Morain is taking us on another journey into the cloud. She has coupled her real-world experience with analytical inputs from industry subject matter experts to clearly articulate a cloud service management model. If you are new to practical cloud implementations, you will find yourself challenging the content. But then you will flip it around and challenge your own views. This is healthy, so remember that Jeanne brings qualitative and quantitative anecdotes and data points that will help you justify your push to the cloud. The cloud is here, and people, machines and applications are using and leveraging it. Your data is moving to the cloud at geometric rates, which is spawning new models like Internet of Things and Industrial Internet, among others. The common thread, however, is the cloud.

As you stand up your cloud, remember you are running a business. Jeanne has done a remarkable job of making you understand the importance of answering critical questions around the business:

- What services you are providing?
- To whom are you providing these services?
- What do your users require to enhance their efforts?

All of these questions seem basic but have dramatic impact when you implement your cloud. Jeanne demonstrates that you must know your target audience, understand that taxonomy is critical to get past any impasses. Traditional IT has changed and the new model is IT as a service provider. While traditionally the idea of customers has been reserved to sales and marketing, IT organizations now also have customers.

These customers are people like you and me. As such we want to know some fundamental facts: What am I getting? Am I getting value from this? As you build your cloud, never forget that you must provide value to your clients. That reality sometimes gets lost in our Agile, Fastworks and other delivery models. Ensure that you have a clearly defined roadmap that includes a constant feedback loop from your customers. Each customer is different. But this book will teach you to clearly define and articulate feature sets applicable to each customer. Customer demands will vary based on cost, security, resiliency, capacity, reliability and performance, and your job will be to translate that into cloud requirements.

Are you ready? If yours is a traditional IT organization, you'll need to change the way you're structured because the implementation of a cloud is an implementation of a new business model. You'll need to drive efforts such as defining the services portfolio and catalog, identifying customer feedback loops and implementing continuous updates/change. Most IT organizations are not structured to handle this new service model and the demands that come with it. If your journey to cloud is to be successful, your IT organizations will have to adapt. You will learn that if organizations do not adapt to the frequency of change and the velocity of change, then people will go out to the cloud themselves — which will require IT to run that data down for the next seven to 10 years. Sound like fun? Didn't think so. What's the best way to avoid that? Plan for the cloud, deploy to the cloud and learn from the cloud! Jeanne's book series will help you navigate the challenges with implementing a successful cloud.

Good luck on your journey.

Brian Cinque

Contents

Introduction

Perception is not always reality for those embarking on the journey to cloud. The road is long, filled with hidden costs and agendas. Similar to the discovery of fire, the emergence of cloud is giving IT organizations a powerful tool. That tool can yield enormous benefits when used correctly, but can create havoc if not understood, contained and used with rules and caution.

Not everyone defines cloud in the same way, which makes understanding and leveraging cloud more difficult. So, to be clear, *iSpeak Cloud* uses the National Institute of Standards and Technology (NIST) definition, which states that a cloud solution must, at a minimum, possess five characteristics: elasticity, pooled resources, depth and breadth of network, self service and measurability. (2011, NIST)

iSpeak Cloud serves as the cloud positioning system that helps you plot coordinates on a map so you can get from where you are today to where you want to be in the future. *iSpeak Cloud: Crossing the Cloud Chasm* provides insights, tips, tricks and approaches for enabling IT organizations to evolve to meet the growing demands of the new *digital native* enterprise.

Why Read This Book?

If your enterprise hasn't already made a conscious choice to adopt cloud solutions, you're in for a big surprise. Your company is there already, at least in terms of having a hybrid cloud.

Hybrid clouds leverage solutions that integrate both internal physical or private cloud solutions with third-party cloud solutions. They come in all shapes and sizes. Salesforce.com® integrated with a back-end tracking and procurement system is one example of a hybrid cloud. A personal Dropbox™ that lets users post content to give a presentation on an Apple iPad™ is another.

While many companies are in the hybrid cloud space, few have consciously embraced it or put policies in place to harness the power or limit the risks. In Gartner Inc.'s 2012 Datacenter Poll,[1] although 45 percent of companies polled indicated they want solutions around hybrid cloud computing, very few had consciously implemented them, and only 31 percent had implemented some form of

---

[1] Mitchel Smith, David, "Hype Cycle for Cloud Computing 2013", Gartner, Inc. 2013

private cloud. Many of the IT professionals interviewed for *iSpeak Cloud* indicated they have been caught off guard by what has become an epidemic facing their companies: Business users are deploying hybrid cloud solutions with or without the company's knowledge.

In *Visible Ops Private Cloud,*[2] my coauthors and I outlined the steps for creating a solid foundation on which to build a private cloud. Many of the interviewees for that book were just beginning to embrace cloud computing and establish policies to build that foundation, so they viewed private cloud as the first step. In my second book, *Client4Cloud,* I expanded on the impact of this shift on the cloud as well as on overall technology adoption. Like gasoline on a fire, the user-centric shift, combined with new regulations around cloud computing, not only fueled widespread adoption of hybrid cloud computing but also introduced additional risks and costs to the enterprise.

Across my three books I have conducted more than 114 interviews with analysts, vendors and enterprise IT professionals. I have been fortunate to be a part of similar major shifts, such as business service management (BSM), regulatory compliance, virtualization and user-centric universal computing. As with these other shifts, the cloud has hit a critical mass stage. And, as with the adoption of cellular technology, cloud consumption with consumerized applications has become an integral part of business as usual.

Unfortunately, the shift is happening so quickly that many enterprises are setting aside good business practices and, as a result, driving up business risk. But slowing the pace is virtually impossible because of the new type of consumer who does not fear technology but embraces it.

Moreover, the dependence on technology is creating an insatiable demand for compelling solutions, automation of repetitive functions and essential cost savings. As companies become more dependent on technology to maintain competitiveness and compliance with regulations, industry standards and corporate policy, IT cannot continue to operate merely as a support organization. Savvy IT organizations are becoming an integral part of delivering compelling solutions that maintain enterprise competitiveness.

---

[2] *Visible Ops Private Cloud: From Virtualization to Cloud in 4 Practical Steps,* Andi Mann, Kurt Milne, and Jeanne Morain, IT Process Institute, 2011. Available from www.itpi.com.

For example, healthcare providers are leveraging scheduling software to reduce wait times in urgent care centers and emergency rooms. Health information exchanges are enabling physicians and their supporting hospital networks to differentiate themselves in care as well as to comply with regulatory mandates. Financial institutions have released competitive differentiators such as mobile deposits to their online banking solutions.

As technology becomes more integral to business success, IT professionals must also evolve their approach from delivering services for the business to consume — such as email or data entry — to managing business solutions and providers. Essentially, for their companies to stay competitive, IT organizations will become the broker of cloud brokers in the interconnected global world.

iSpeak Cloud will help you drive this transformation in your enterprise. *iSpeak Cloud* provides best practices for enhancing your company's policies, skills and strategy around embracing the shift to cloud while minimizing risk and keeping costs in check. As with other paradigm shifts, the winners will be the enterprises that embrace the change. Those that resist it will be lucky to survive.

Thriving on Change

Google is a perfect example of a company that thrives on change. In response to early predictions of mobility, consumerization of IT and other trends, management quickly expanded Google's initial scope as a search engine company to fields encompassing mobility, online chat, global positioning systems and other related areas. Google solutions capitalize on being the fabric that ties together highly social and mobile digital native users. This approach helped the company thrive while early competitors Infoseek, Webcrawler and Ask Jeeves floundered.

Understanding the Cloud Chasm

The *cloud chasm* is the gap between where the enterprise believes it needs to be with respect to cloud-based technology and IT's ability to deliver solutions across various clouds, devices and users while balancing business requirements, compliance and resource availability. The gap is widening because employees — not only from the business side but also from the IT side — are rapidly adopting solutions outside of the control, scope and understanding of IT. A number of factors are motivating them to circumvent IT, including:

- The ability to charge inexpensive, cloud-based consumer solutions to a credit card
- Technically savvy business people who are looking to improve work/life balance
- Growing number of regulations and standards around technology for audit and compliance
- Shortage of resources in IT, which causes implementation delays
- Brownfield solutions that need to be augmented, integrated or replaced
- Lack of a common language between IT and the business, leading to miscommunication and adversarial relationships

IT professionals are struggling to address the resulting clash in the cloud, which Figure 1 illustrates.

Figure 1. Factors contributing to today's clash in the cloud.

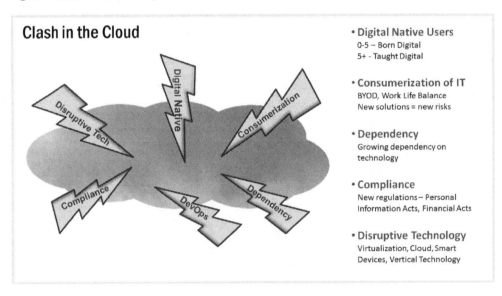

Business users are actively embracing the consumerization of IT trends such as bring your own device (BYOD) partly because they typically have not only their corporate-issued laptops or personal computers but also tablets and smartphones. These devices increase employee satisfaction and productivity, and, in the case of smart devices, decrease costs. However, they also open the door to noncompliance with regulatory requirements and/or corporate policy if people use personal storage devices or other devices to access protected information or company intellectual property (IP).

As business people continue to circumvent the IT organization to implement new tools, create custom tools that augment or work around a specific solution and leverage software-as-a-service (SaaS) solutions, the shadow IT environment expands. Because shadow IT is outside the jurisdiction of IT, it hampers IT's ability to protect corporate data and IP and ensure compliance.

Here are two examples. One company interviewed for this book discovered more than 300 rogue SaaS applications and other shadow solutions during a cloud security audit. In another company, an IT group convinced a business unit to authorize the implementation of an entire solution on a third-party public cloud. When an internal audit found it, the group was forced to bring the solution in house primarily because the third party did not encrypt the data at rest. Serious business risks were involved with respect to the security of the systems and data. Moreover, the true up of accounting expenses clearly showed that cloud does not always equate to savings.

Both cases underscore the big divide in understanding and acumen for both technology risks to the business and business risks to technology. More often than not, it's a breakdown in communication that perpetuates the great divide. This is in part due to different viewpoints or camps that have not evolved fast enough to keep up with the changing world around them. It's similar to the evolution from the floppy drive to the CD or from physical to virtual systems. It takes more than technology change for innovation to work. People and supporting processes must also adapt and evolve.

As with strained marriages, both business and technology are approaching the problem from different perspectives. Both think they know the right answer. Ironically, both are partially right. Business users historically understand what it takes to run the company and the history of how things have evolved over time. The IT staff knows more about the back-end systems and technically how things are architected. And both have misconceptions about what is and is not acceptable for the other to adopt as an interim solution.

The cloud chasm exists because of people and process issues more so than issues related to the underlying technology. Companies that have immature processes typically suffer from strained relationships between IT and the business. As a result, they tend to have a deeper and wider chasm. Companies with more mature processes and a deeper understanding of the technology have been able to harness more of the benefits of hybrid cloud from a cost and competitive agility perspective. The one key attribute of those that are able to cross the cloud chasm and those that fall into the abyss is the ability to communicate or translate requirements of the business and technology to create compelling solutions.

Figure 2 summarizes some of the major causes of the cloud chasm and offers solutions for getting to the root of the problem and solving it.

Figure 2. Causes and solutions of the cloud chasm.

Chasm Causes	Examples	Solution To Cross Chasm
Shadow IT Business and technology leveraging SaaS or cloud solutions without IT's knowledge	• Even our developers were expensing Amazon virtual machines without our knowledge, driving up our OpEx costs. • The business worked around IT and funded a SaaS start up. • Our cloud OpEx was 75 percent higher than budgeted during mid-year audit because business and IT users were expensing third-party VM solutions on corporate credit cards	• Create policies and avenues to allow use of preferred third-party clouds. • Work with business to create and enforce policies that enable safe usage with preferred providers.
Consumerization of IT and BYOD Consumer apps and devices are being leveraged to work around IT with or without the approval of the business	• We had to block access to Dropbox to reduce security risks. But users adopted other solutions for personal storage, so all we did was shift the risk. • Our CEO purchased iPads for senior managers without consulting IT. We had to purchase enterprise Dropbox and quickly identify policies on how to support these users.	• Create policies on consumer device usage specifying which devices are acceptable and which are not. • Create security restrictions via software to enable wiping devices of company IP. • Educate both business and technology leadership about risks of unmanaged solutions.
DevOps (Continuous Delivery) Development and operations working to accelerate delivery of production updates on a frequent basis	• Continuous delivery works great for mature products but we get pushback from the business on large-scale rollouts due to risks. • The project was halted after a major outage caused by a quick hit into production that neither the support desk nor business was prepared to handle.	• Create and agree upon an iterative, agile quarterly delivery cadence (2 major, 2 minor) with business stakeholders. • Ensure organizational change management is involved in any user-facing changes. • Institute release to production checklist for minimum viable testing prior to implementing.

Agile Costing Methods — Agile development models make it harder to predict and create accurate cost models for business case approvals	• Project costs were 2x-3x higher than anticipated with no clear end in sight. We're afraid our execs will kill it. • Financial Planning & Analysis having a hard time costing portfolios due to limited information. • We learned a hard lesson about OpEx and CapEx when we spent millions on a SaaS solution that took years to deploy to scale. • Lack of costing resulted in bad behaviors, "attaching costs" to wrong projects as the projects were either underfunded or could not get funding.	• Right size portfolio delivery method and costing to the project (Kanban Agile, Iterative Agile or Waterfall). • Implement process and method to build out costs at least 12-18 months in advance. • Work with business to understand time to value, scale and timelines. • Educate and hold managers accountable for their profit-and-loss margins on their portfolios.

Building the Bridge

Crossing the cloud chasm starts with building a bridge with the business by understanding what benefit or value business users are seeking, how IT is either meeting the needs or not and educating stakeholders on solutions.

Bridges are not built overnight. The task is more difficult in companies that have:

- Created processes and adopted technologies that worked well in the past, but are no longer serving the needs of the business
- Adopted new processes prescribed by a vendor or hyped up as an industry trend without taking the needs of the business into account

I learned about the difficulties of building bridges in the early days of business service management, a discipline that emerged in 2002. BSM was not intended to be purely about the plumbing or managing the underlying systems or infrastructure. Instead, the concept centered on working hand-in-hand with the business to create services that address enterprise needs. Those of us involved in the evolution of BSM likened it to creating a blueprint for a house. Just as the blueprint for a house has to include all the elements of the house, an IT service blueprint has to include all elements of the service and take into account the needs of the customer. So as you build your business service foundation it is essential to look at the layers in the stack, shown in Figure 3, and define the service from the customer (business) perspective.

Figure 3. Layers of the BSM operational stack.

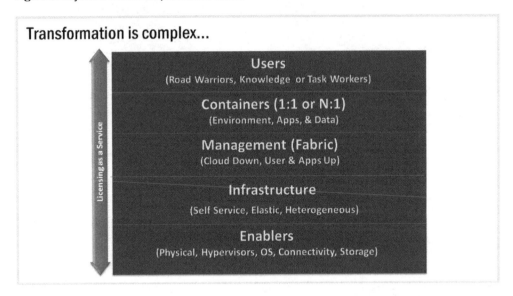

BSM created a solid framework for standardizing processes across the operational stack. As a result, many operational teams have a good model or way to calculate and control costs for distributing and maintaining the underlying plumbing. While this transformation helped IT evolve, it was the tip of the iceberg in the evolution that continues today in defining a clear business service that meets the objectives of the business.

The BSM blueprint we started with defines a clear way to create a solid foundation that ensures change management and infrastructure management can accommodate the growing demands of the business. The missing link was the bridge between the services or applications that are being consumed by both the business and its customers to provide competitive advantage in the marketplace. Without solid processes and without a clear understanding of how to bridge the next layer in the service for the company, the business (along with its digital native employees) has adopted and adapted to get what people need to succeed — with or without IT's support. This has created a divide between business and IT, in some cases creating a virtual chasm that is fueled by readily available and relatively inexpensive SaaS and cloud-based solutions.

Many of the people interviewed for this book cited two types of challenges: not being able to get the requirements from the business, and having business leaders adopt and implement solutions without IT having a seat at the table. As a result, regardless of how many consultants were brought on board or how many leading technologies were purchased, projects were only moderately successful at best. In many cases, projects were over budget or failed all together.

Many of the projects described by interviewees were characterized by politics, blame games and infighting. In at least one case, the CEO funded a startup to remove the "IT factor" from the mix and have more control over costs and delivery. It seems like a drastic measure, but the motivating factor was frustration and miscommunication. IT and the business had spent millions of dollars over a three-year period without solving the business challenges or having a concrete solution in hand. Unfortunately, the startup approach was not successful because the SaaS solution created security and compliance risks. Additionally, the IT staff had to get involved anyway to assist with legacy integration. The business gained more control, but in the end the costs were not contained and there were numerous bottlenecks and delays because the project was not budgeted or supported originally as part of the overall IT plan.

In another company, the chief information officer (CIO) and the chief operating officer (COO) hired competing audit firms to prove to each other that the implementation was not addressing the pain points in the business case. The program was over budget and behind schedule. Both the business and technology leaders blamed each other for the failures. The real culprit, however, was the communication breakdown. Both executives believed they knew more about the types of solutions needed. The business leader purchased technical solutions and hired technical staff to deploy, update and maintain them in third-party clouds.

This duplication of effort drove up overall program costs. The unfortunate outcome was that the rogue implementation not only cost the company 75 percent more than original estimates, but also it fell short of meeting the business requirements because the business leader failed to select purpose-built solutions.

The lesson to learn from both examples is that although business people understand their requirements better than anyone in the company, chances are they lack a deep knowledge of the technology landscape. The converse is also true. The IT staff understands the technology but typically lacks knowledge with respect to the business requirements.

Another factor that disrupts communication between the business and IT is that today's business users are far more tech savvy. Many of the people coming of age in business are digital natives. They learned to use technology when they were learning to walk and talk. While their digitally taught counterparts were willing to be locked out or locked down for their own good or have their technology needs dictated, the digital natives will not stand for this. Moreover, while they will not consciously put the company at risk, they will tweet, copy, paste and save to do their jobs without giving a second thought to whether or not they are violating some regulation or written IT policy.

So where do you start with respect to building a bridge? Bridge building typically starts with changing who is invited to the table when the business is looking for solutions to a problem. Senior technology leaders will be able to gain a seat at the table only if they regain the trust of the business, create policies that build in flexibility with compliance and start to list the business service requirements.

During my time as a troubleshooter for early adopters of BSM, I learned that the single most crippling factor preventing success was the failure to listen. Both sides are typically at fault, and the cost of the failure to communicate is high. Implementing solutions, like building new products for the market, costs more the farther down the line the gaps are allowed to travel. Figure 4 "does the math" and shows the cost of catching a missed requirement at various stages. Once you're in production, the cost in terms of dollars and time to address it rises to 100 times.

Figure 4. The cost of fixing a missed requirement.

If requirements defects are:	Then costs are:
Discovered in design	1 x
Discovered in testing or development	10x
Discovered in production with the customer	100x

How Top Performers Get it Done

Too often, despite the cost implications, complexity and time to value, companies don't invest enough time in planning to gain clarity. The top-performing companies interviewed for this book spent more time in planning and less in delivery and execution than their lower-performing counterparts. As one interviewee put it so well, "To truly go fast you have to slow down and create a plan first, instead of just running ahead."

The CIOs of companies that have successfully crossed the cloud chasm have several common characteristics:

- **Facilitation**. They facilitate a seat at the table for key stakeholders across business, technology and governance.
- **Guard rails not roadblocks**. Instead of creating roadblocks that stop business users, they create and enforce policies and governance models that guide them.
- **Emphasis on planning.** They require business cases that reflect return on equity across the lifespan of equivalent applications for the company as input in their overall decision making and strategy.
- **Accountability**. They hold both business and technology teams accountable for their plans around project profits or savings from the product implementation.
- **Embraced change.** Rarely are they caught in the hype cycle, nor are they bleeding-edge adopters. However, they are often in the first 15 to 20 percent of companies to adopt compelling technologies, processes or methodologies.

Top-performing CIOs know the space they serve and the technologies in the market — particularly technologies that are as far reaching and impactful as cloud. Lower-performing companies, on the other hand, often confuse cloud with server virtualization or SaaS applications hosted at someone else's site.

Leaders across IT and the business must work together to cross the cloud chasm. Although every company's transformation will be unique depending on goals, current maturity level and culture, there are five common steps that top-performing companies take to transform current processes, skills and tools and embrace the user-centric paradigm shift across the various layers in the stack from the infrastructure to the application. Figure 5 summarizes the steps and the goals of each one. The remainder of this book dives deeper into each area to illustrate what transformation success looks like.

Figure 5. The Five Steps Top Performers Use to Cross the Cloud Chasm.

Step	Description	Goal
1	Define Cloud Command and Control Center (who, what, why, when, how)	Create executive-level governance board of cross-functional business leaders to define the transformation strategy and policies.
2	Roadmap to Cloud	Identify key pain points for the business to solve, then define and align people, process and technology needed to address them based on qualitative and quantitative metrics.

3	Calculate Cloud Costs and Compliance (portfolio)	Assess, enhance and/or implement portfolio (product, service, solution) management processes at lower levels that can cover costing across development models and take compliance (business, security, regulatory) to key directives into account.
4	Calibrate Cloud Vision to Reality (illustrate, integrate, iterate)	Assign portfolio leaders and workstreams to align executive vision (the desired state) to reality (the current state). Goals of the team should include illustrating the gaps, integrating to workstreams and brownfield solutions, and iterative planning from vision to reality based on costs and overall benefit to the company.
5	Execute and Evaluate (KPIs, services, improve)	Execute and evaluate approved portfolio plans by the governance oversight board. Evaluate the identified key performance indicators early and often to feed into continuous improvement and discontinue projects that fail to meet the desired state outcomes.

The hardest part of crossing the chasm is breaking down the silos that separate not only IT and the business but also those that isolate individual IT groups and prevent them from working as a team. Companies that have struggled the hardest to address internal political pitfalls report higher numbers of shadow IT applications and an inability to execute. The key goal of top management is to pull all the teams together and avoid the typical business-versus-technology political posturing. For the culture to truly embrace the changes ahead, management must ensure that the leader of each group of stakeholders has a seat at the table and that translators are available for them so they can come to understand each other's perspectives. For management to achieve what is truly the best thing for the company, compromise is inevitable.

This is an area that the technology industry has struggled with since the 1990s when Carly Fiorina of HP first took the stage and talked about eliminating the silos in IT. Although we have come a long way, we still have a long way to go. This is due in part to human factors and in part to the established culture of many older companies. Older companies with strongly engrained cultures will struggle harder to make the transformation. The benefits of a successful transformation, however, will be enormous.

- Cleaning the cloud wash. *Cloud washing* is the practice of rebranding products to incorporate the term *cloud* whether or not the product was purpose built for the cloud. This practice makes cutting through the hype and clutter around cloud a nearly insurmountable task. Learn more about the *iSpeak Cloud* recipe for eliminating cloud wash.
- While virtualization works as a catalyst in creating a more efficient, scalable and dynamic cloud environment, virtualization in and of itself is not the same thing as cloud. Learn more about the relationship between virtualization and cloud.

Setting the Stage

iSpeak Cloud is based on hours of interviews with dozens of IT leaders who shared real-world scenarios and best practices. The book leverages these inputs, blending fiction and nonfiction to provide a practical guide to many of the challenges companies face today when they try to implement a cohesive cloud strategy that promotes corporate directives related to such areas as security, regulatory and the business.

To illustrate the challenges and offer guidance on overcoming them, *iSpeak Cloud* uses an imaginary company that is representative of the many companies who participated in the research. Universal Kingdom is a Fortune 2000 international medical service provider and the holding company for a diverse portfolio of provider services from medical to banking and financial services. Universal Kingdom has a robust portfolio of subsidiaries that range from financial services to fund/exchange financing payments, to arranging medical tourism, providing medical education/tutorials and providing medical billing services. As such, the company has a diverse set of requirements around products, services and regulatory compliance.

Newly hired CIO Charles Eubanks has four fundamental objectives that he will be measured against:

1. *Increasing time to value* of key business initiatives affecting market competitiveness

2. *Providing transparency* for the board around profit and loss of the current technology portfolio investments
3. *Addressing compliance concerns* raised by audit
4. *Reducing IT spend* by 30 percent to keep the business running

Building the Cloud Governance Team

During his first eight weeks on the job, Charles has been trying to evaluate and understand the players, gaps in skills sets and maturity level of the organization, and to create an overarching strategy to move forward. Over the years, Charles has turned to mentors and colleagues in the industry for advice and to serve as a sounding board for formulating a strategy. Charles' informal advisory team consists of industry luminaries, thought leaders and board members.

Throughout his journey to the cloud, Charles will rely upon the advice, articles and quotes of these people to guide him on the road to success. He will also rely on the experience he gained working for one of the first companies to adopt BSM. That experience taught him that it's what you don't know that has the biggest impact on the overall success of the implementation. It also taught him that when key people either do not have a seat at the table or are consulted too late in the process, the results are higher costs and lengthy implementation cycles.

So Charles knows that his first step must be to assemble a team of internal experts who have the right blend of expertise on Universal Kingdom's business directives (company, regulatory, security) as well as on the available cloud technologies to enable those directives.

As he considered the various candidates, Charles recalled an interesting Forrester report stating that more than 50 percent of company projects involved cloud computing and that, although the majority of business stakeholders believed IT should drive cloud policy, many would circumvent IT to adopt cloud solutions.[3] The primary reasons cited were to the need for self service, ease of use and time to value.

Charles was worried he would find himself facing the same troublesome situation so many of his peers were reporting. Despite having rigorous cloud policies in place, these IT professionals were reporting that business users — and even IT

---

[3] "Your Cloud Future is Here: How IT Can Embrace The Business Demand for Cloud and Exceed Expectations." Forrester Consulting, 2013.

groups — were implementing cloud solutions without IT's input or knowledge. One colleague had uncovered hundreds of applications purchased by various business managers.

It was clear that the best way to get buy-in from business leaders would be to ensure that the right business stakeholders were heavily involved in discussions about cloud usage policies. That meant identifying key executives from major facets of the business and inviting them to participate. He did not want to invite too many, however, because when a team exceeds 15 people, the risk of analysis paralysis is high and might prevent Charles from accomplishing goals set out by the board.

Another area of concern for Charles is overall governance and compliance. As an international company, Universal Kingdom has to worry about legislation and regulations that vary from country to country. European countries, for example, insist that the data their employees use be hosted within the borders of the country in which they work.

To bring this type of expertise to the team, Charles included not only a member of the audit and compliance team, but also someone from legal. Compliance, after all, is critical given how regulated the financial services and medical industries are.

Charles remembered reading about new guidelines being created by NIST around cloud computing. He needed someone who could not only audit but make sure that Universal Kingdom complied with these standards. One way to really cut costs is to avoid redo work due to lack of compliance. For these reasons Charles decided he needed the participation of three key roles: the chief information security officer, general counsel or member from her team, and the head of technology audit. The latter, Charles was sure, had learned quite a bit from initial audit efforts and had a vested interest in helping him create best practices.

With the players for the business, security, legal and compliance teams identified, Charles turned his attention to the technical team. Although technology leadership participation was critical, Charles also wanted strong representation from the people tasked with doing the work. For this reason he asked each member of his leadership team to appoint a star player from each area. This would ensure that the new policies would balance executive oversight and employee input, thereby increasing the probability of adoption. That would mean that he would need representation from development leadership, architects and operations across both client and data center.

One thing Charles knew firsthand was that without accountability and ownership, the probability of success would be low. For this cloud initiative to take off, Charles would need to tightly manage the swim lanes and understand the rollout strategy. It would take a strong team of executives to create the policy, and a strong team of experts to execute it. Universal Kingdom leveraged IT Infrastructure Library (ITIL) guidelines and was looking to evolve its BSM approach. The company was big on agile development best practices and BSM. He would need to appoint a special product owners group (SPOG) to ensure that, from planning to architecture to final implementation, all facets would be carefully thought through and enforced.

The SPOG would consist of three key roles: the cloud architect, the cloud program manager and a new role cloud portfolio leader (also known as business service manager). The product portfolio leader would be responsible for not only helping to define the cloud strategy but also ensuring that the company had captured the critical requirements for creating and implementing overarching cloud policies and solutions.

Cast of Characters

With a clear idea about who would be at the table, Charles assembled the team to determine the company's current state of cloud readiness. He scheduled a three-day offsite meeting of the key stakeholders, whom he identified as having the ability to create a balanced cloud strategy. The organizational chart in Figure lists these stakeholders and shows the reporting structure of each one up through the company's chief executive officer.

The remainder of this book uses a workshop approach that puts you, the reader, in the middle of the action. Identify the character that most closely aligns with your role in your enterprise and join the members of Universal Kingdom's newly formed cloud governance team.

Listen in on Kayla Coletrain's presentations, tips, advice and examples and find out what your colleagues have to say about the issues that are important to them. At the end of each session, read through the "Food for Thought" section and spend a few minutes considering how closely the interactions align with what might happen in your enterprise. Think about how the interactions and tasks might differ based on your industry, organizational structure and IT environment.

Through your virtual participation in this workshop, you'll experience firsthand how a team can work together to set aside hidden agendas and political maneuvering and engage in productive interactions, idea sharing and problem solving.

[Continued on next page]

Figure 6. Key members of Universal Kingdom's Cloud Governance Committee.

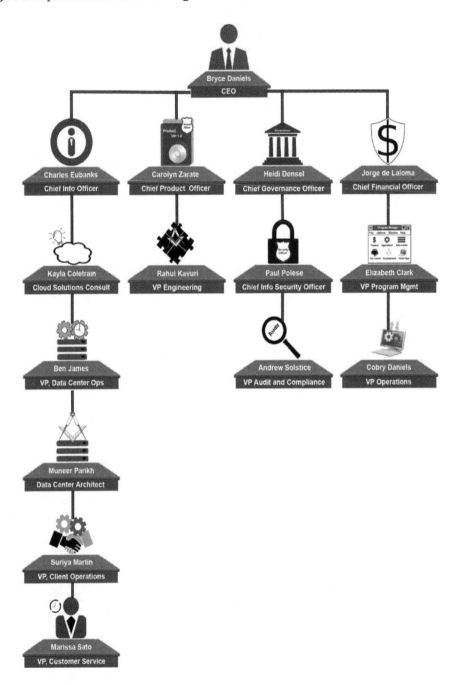

Cloud Quest Workshop Day 1

Morning Session: Creating Cloud Command and Control

Objectives

Define and clarify roles, responsibilities, rules, process and accountability for Universal Kingdom's Cloud Command and Control team.

Session Background/Overview

Universal Kingdom has seen delays in its overall cloud execution strategy. These delays have had a domino effect on other key initiatives around customer relationship management and unified communication solutions. The purpose of this session is get back on track. By the end of Day 1, you will understand:

- What a cohesive cloud execution team should look like
- Who typically is invited to the table
- The key objectives and responsibilities to be considered
- Tradeoffs that must be understood and in place before the strategy is complete
- How to lay the ground rules of engagement across the IT silos

The Action

(Charles kicks off the meeting with some introductory remarks and then encourages the team to participate.)

ⓘ Charles   Good morning. First and foremost, thank you for attending today's kickoff of our cloud governance workshop. Let me start by getting everyone on the same page with respect to what we're going to accomplish over the next three days. I've summarized our goals in the slide you see here.

Workshop Objectives
- Assess the current state
- Create harmonistic approach for cloud deployments
- Identify/address requirements and risks
- Enforce/enhance policies on an ongoing basis

First, we need to understand what's going on today with respect to cloud computing at Universal Kingdom. I'm talking about rising IT costs and the cloud stall we're seeing because we don't have a comprehensive cloud strategy.

Second, we want to create a harmonistic approach and policy for deploying cloud-based solutions across business and technology.

Third, we must identify and address requirements and risks for deploying cloud solutions at Universal Kingdom.

And fourth, we want to enforce policies during the pilot, as well as during the creation and ongoing execution of cloud solutions, to meet corporate goals with respect to growth and performance. And we want to ensure that we have a process in place to continuously improve our cloud strategy to get the most out of our investment in cloud solutions.

This next slide summarizes what I believe we have to do to achieve these goals.

Universal Kingdom Cloud Governance

Method for Achieving Objectives

- Brainstorm ideas for bringing current cloud efforts under control
- Agree on compelling strategies for deployment
- Define KPIs
- Hold stakeholders accountable for pilot, deployment and enforcement

Number 1, once we've figured out where we are with respect to cloud readiness, we need to come up with ideas for overcoming the obstacles that are preventing us from developing a sound cloud strategy.

Number 2, we've got to clearly assign, define and realign seats at the table to create and agree on compelling strategies for deploying cloud solutions.

Three, define key performance indicators, including savings and anticipated return on equity, for creating cloud policies.

And four, define overall objectives, meeting cadence and requirements of this governance team in holding accountable the people responsible for pilot, deployment and enforcement.

Muneer, can you provide more of an overview on what our current state of cloud readiness is?

 Muneer
Yes, sir. Well, like most companies, our current state is predicated on server virtualization with some management framework applied. We haven't quite integrated our implementation of cloud technology with our configuration management database. As a result, although we have quite a few virtualized

> **Current state**: Virtualized applications. Limited and very manual management.

applications, our management of them is still very manual and limited at best.

Paul   Muneer, in your summary, where do you account for third-party cloud providers and the SaaS applications that are currently being used? Because, during our recent cloud audit, we identified over 300 applications that were not on IT's authorized list. We tracked a lot of them down to monthly expense or personal accounts across both IT and the business.

Muneer   Unfortunately, this architectural specification doesn't include SaaS or third-party infrastructure-as-a-service solutions. We do account for our own internal framework and managed services that run on that framework. Were you expecting the data center engineering team to address this issue?

Charles   If not the data center team, who would own the monitoring of these third-party solutions? Client operations? Or the IT operations center? Do we know who authorized them, and how can we ensure this doesn't keep happening?

Paul   Well, Charles, you authorized some of them. Remember last Christmas when you purchased iPads for all the senior leaders? Well, they needed a way to view data and presentations, so they started to use Dropbox. Other applications, for example, the configuration solution that was purchased, are part of our production systems and integrate into our online CRM solution. Some of the add-ons are enhancements to improve performance or enable moving up our development and test deployment cycles from what the report states.

> **Unpleasant surprises:** Senior leaders may be copying sensitive data onto third-party clouds, introducing significant risk.

Heidi   Paul, did I hear you correctly? Are you saying we knowingly allowed regulated financial and protected data to be copied off our network onto third-party clouds? I highly doubt any of us here thought using our iPads would put the company at risk. How quickly can we rectify this situation and get everyone off those applications?

Paul   Wait a second, Heidi, that only solves part of the problem. We don't have any projects or budget items approved to remediate or replace these 300 applications. Do we even have an idea of how much it would cost to remediate something like that, or to what extent these applications are in use?

Do you remember how much time it took and how hard it was to identify the unauthorized spend on third-party clouds that people were charging on their corporate cards? Turned out we were using only 2,000 out of the 5,000 instances that were auto-charging. That was an expensive proposition all the way around, and we still need to decommission several of these systems.

Carolyn   Everyone, we need to take a deep breath and take a step back. Obviously there are quite a few factors contributing to our risks here. We didn't get into this mess overnight and it will take time to fix things. The key is determining the best way to balance our portfolio and reduce the highest risk with the most cost savings first. It's imperative that we take baby steps here.

Rahul   Whoa there, Carolyn. Remember we are an agile development shop and have invested quite a bit in implementing DevOps solutions to increase the velocity of solution delivery across our business entities. What you are saying sounds very "waterfall" in approach. I don't support any approach that would significantly impact our ability to execute, given the growing market demand for our products.

Charles   Rahul, we're not talking about moving away from agile or DevOps. How come every time we suggest any change that restricts engineering to reduce risk or the impact on customers, it becomes an agile discussion? Seriously, we all understand agile is a critical component of what we do, but let's not muddy the waters here.

Let's bring this discussion back to the objectives I laid out at the beginning of this workshop. The bottom line is the current state of cloud adoption has and will continue to have a negative impact on every single department in this company unless we get ahead of it.

And we can't get ahead of it unless every one of us is willing to put aside any hidden agendas and quit tearing each other down. If we're going to succeed in today's dependent technology world, we have to embrace the change that cloud represents before it gets any further out of control.

> **Key to containing costs/minimizaing risk:** Put aside hidden agendas and collaborate across functional areas.

Now, I've asked Kayla Coletrain to join us to figure out how we can apply best practices to rein in our initiatives around cloud computing.

Kayla comes highly recommended by our board for her work around BSM and cloud strategies. As the rest of you probably know, Carolyn led the project for Kayla to analyze our current state of cloud readiness and risk. Kayla, can you give us some insight on the challenges we are facing? On a scale of one to ten where would you say we are on a maturity level?

Kayla   This may not be what you want to hear, but Universal is on the lower end of the maturity scale when it comes to cloud. Having said that, please note that you are not alone. Many companies are in the same boat. This is partially due to the nascent nature of the technology and best practices. And it's partially due to cloud confusion caused by marketing hype, lack of policies and the current state of the company.

Any major initiative or shift requires strong, cohesive leadership so that the change delivers positive results. In any organization, no matter how great each individual silo is at picking technology, it's the people and process, and the collaboration across silos that determine if the technology will deliver positive outcomes.

Technology, no matter where it's located or what you call it, can bring very positive change and help the company prosper if applied with the right processes by people with the right skills. Or it can have the opposite effect. It really boils down to what business value the company is hoping to achieve by implementing this new cloud service.

How many of you have heard about the hybrid cloud hydra conundrum?

(Kayla pulls up a slide illustrating the cloud hydra conundrum.)

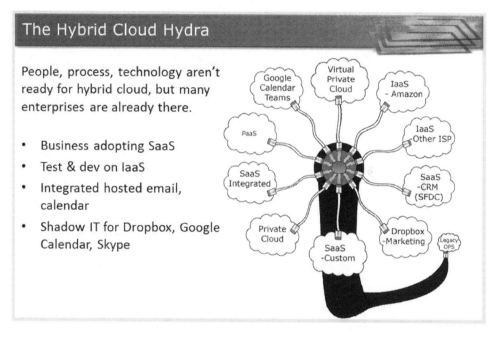

Paul: Isn't that when the current state of cloud adoption has outpaced the policies, procedures and processes in place to manage it. So, a company grows, and maybe there are mergers and acquisitions. People start implementing solutions across public and private, virtual and physical infrastructures. You get people putting in SaaS solutions in silos without a cohesive strategy. Each component is like an individual head of the hydra. Each one is consuming resources and time. In our case, one of the heads of the hydra is that we have thousands of people using Dropbox instead of the company-sponsored application.

Muneer: We have lots of shadow IT activities going on, with the business working around IT and procuring technology that IT then has to integrate into existing systems. Because we aren't 100 percent in one infrastructure or another, it creates a fragmented approach.

Most of these projects don't follow architectural best practices around data center optimization. The business users are pretty technically savvy, but they don't fully understand all the critical-path components we have to put in place for security, disaster recovery, monitoring and business continuity across not just systems but networks.

Kayla Those are great examples of the hybrid cloud hydra and the problems it introduces. The truth for many companies is that they already have a hybrid cloud implementation whether or not they want it. Similar to the multiheaded serpent of Greek mythology, the hybrid cloud hydra has huge impacts for the enterprise on costs, compliance and business risk.

The hydra takes over without anybody realizing it. You have all these different groups creating business cases and authorizing projects within the confines of their respective silos. And please don't blame it all on business users, because IT groups are doing the same thing. The problem is, the business cases don't take into account the resources, costs and policies needed across future and current systems — both within the company's domain and in third-party domains.

Elizabeth An example might help us understand this a little better.

Kayla Sure. So, let's say you're implementing an online customer relationship management solution. You can't do it in a vacuum. You already have a lot of internal systems and data sources that you should leverage, so you can get the most out of the CRM system. Accounting, customer data, bulk email or client email applications, or unified communications solutions. You need unique skills and a deep understanding of the company's current solutions to successfully implement a SaaS CRM solution.

Now let's talk about how the hydra affects each of you. It creates contention for the critical resources that have both a deep understanding of the environment and a solid understanding of the technologies involved. If you underestimate the need for those resources, I can almost guarantee you that things won't end well.

Resource contention causes delays in other projects, and it introduces compliance risks because you may end up relying on consultants or lower-skilled staff trying to fill the void. There's also a bigger risk of overstated business cases that cut company staff too deeply without enough people left to implement the new technology or support existing systems.

> **Hydra impact:**
> Contention among functional areas delays projects and introduces compliance risks as employees are tasked with responsibilities they don't have the skills to handle.

Other side effects include business units trying to circumvent IT through outsourcing more of the role. But the error here is not knowing what the impact will be in terms of network traffic, latency for users, business continuity and planning. This is something that I like to call *cloud dynamics,* which is understanding and having a plan to address the downstream and upstream impacts to the business if something in the integrated network across the layers in the stack is affected. Companies with well-defined processes and the right mix of skills needed to support the solution typically have a strong understanding of impact.

But moving to a dynamic environment that combines multiple layers in the stack without policies, processes and support for the underlying technology is like pouring gasoline on a fire. Just because you can doesn't mean you should, as it may burn hotter than you intended. What I'm saying is this: The dynamic nature of the cloud will highlight and point out gaps in people, process and technology, which brings me to my next slide.

This slide touches on one of my favorite examples, the Netflix™ and Amazon incident that happened around Christmas of 2012.

 Marissa   I remember that. What a nightmare for Netflix customer service. People were so mad about the disruption to streaming video.

Kayla   What a lot of people don't know is that one year prior to this highly publicized outage, Amazon had another outage that affected a handful of smaller customers. Many of them were outraged but few would take responsibility for the fact that they didn't have a business continuity or disaster recovery plan in place in the event of an Amazon issue. If you're running mission-critical applications in a cloud, it doesn't matter if that cloud is on premise or run by a third party, you need a business continuity plan. We have to keep in mind that cloud

> **Business Continuity:**
>
> If you're running mission-critical applications in a cloud — on premise or third party — you're responsible for business continuity/disaster recovery.

providers are data center providers. As such, they can be hit with network, hardware or software issues when their environment is overloaded or hardware fails. Having a plan for that eventuality is the responsibility of the company that is using that third-party provider.

Ben, can you tell us if we have anything in place today in case there's a failure or outage with our infrastructure provider?

 Ben

Our network operations center has tools that monitor the performance of infrastructure-as-a-service solutions across our cloud, and those tools provide aggregated dashboards on whether the third-party solutions are up or down and how well they are meeting their service levels. Because we use a virtual private cloud with Amazon, we have our agents installed on those VMs and an appliance that reports back on performance for updates.

Kayla

Why did you choose to use your existing monitoring tools instead of a solution that is already offered on Amazon?

Ben

Because it's integrated into our systems and helps us identify points of failure across service solutions. We tried some third-party monitoring tools, but it was hard to justify with our current investments on the solution we have built out. And the entire team understands how to use what we have. Adding another application only complicates things and makes it harder for Tier 2 support to troubleshoot. Besides, many of the tools we looked at only provided a partial solution. For example, we could get IaaS monitoring but not integrated with our SaaS vendors. Many of our existing tools can give us IaaS by adding a reverse proxy and hub on the cloud provider. The benefits compared to the costs simply are not there.

Kayla

Rahul, your team heads up a large SaaS implementation for CRM. Can you tell me how you utilize this monitoring solution across the stack?

Rahul Sure, we had Ben add a ping to the current monitoring solution so if our SaaS provider goes down, we are alerted.

Kayla Interesting. Carolyn, how is this meeting your needs?

Carolyn It isn't really. We know whether the site is up or not, but we don't know why we're experiencing latency issues with some of our applications or why certain features of the application are not working. We get lots of ideas and suggestions, but it always takes much longer to identify the root cause and actually address the issue than what we experienced with the on-premise solution we used to have. Honestly, poor Marissa's team gets hammered when there's a service issue because it's like finding a needle in a haystack.

Muneer This is exactly the gap I was mentioning earlier to Paul. Sure, we understand whether the service is up or down but not much more.

Marissa This is why we feel like we need more autonomy to go directly with a third-party vendor. When we call IT regarding the issues, it takes so long to resolve an issue and, in some cases, it never gets resolved. As a business leader, what am I supposed to do when the application running our call center isn't working? I have to tell employees to let customers know the system is down and ask them to call back later. It really impacts our overall customer and employee satisfaction. This has been a huge issue for us not only when the site is down, but also when it is not working properly. At least with a third-party vendor it sounds like it would be easier to resolve the issue.

Rahul Marissa, we've had this discussion previously. When your solution provider goes down, what is your business continuity plan?

Marissa The provider will handle all that in the service level agreement. It's the cloud, they have that taken care of.

Rahul   That would only be the case if we were not integrating to so many of our back-end legacy systems. A lot is depending on our solutions, and if we can't holistically monitor the entire service, it makes it difficult to track issues across the layers in the stack — the applications, networks, storage and users. The reason IT takes so much longer is that putting this larger puzzle together takes time, and each area needs to be tested to ensure we are not breaking production.

Kayla   Let's stop here and reflect on this discussion before it digresses too far. You are all right. But you all have to work together to solve the problem. What you're experiencing here is known as a *cloud chasm*. As you see in this next slide, the chasm occurs when the business is working around IT and going directly to the provider because the provider's solutions address their pain points.

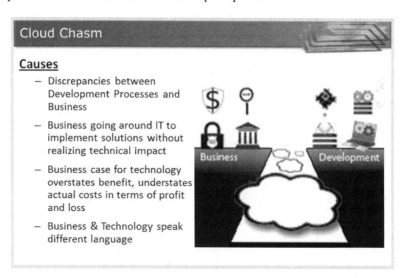

IT needs to integrate these solutions to provide the same or a higher level of service to meet SLAs, but the current budget, skill sets and tools needed around monitoring, compliance and workload balancing have not caught up to the requirements. In essence, there is a chasm between what the business needs and the solutions IT can provide. The good news is you are not alone. Many Fortune 2000 companies are facing this same challenge. What is widening the gap is the fact that from an IT perspective you are still a technology provider, but the business is asking for solutions to their service requirements.

 Ben   This is making sense. What do we do?

Kayla   One of the things we will achieve in this workshop is to figure out, as a team, what are the essential elements to crossing the cloud chasm. And we're going to leave here as a team with actionable plans, policies and insight into gaps in procedures. In short, we're leaving here with what we need to set leadership up for success.

Look, it's clear from the discussion that the biggest obstacle keeping Universal Kingdom from moving to a higher level of cloud maturity isn't a lack of technology. You own products from many of the leading solution providers. What you're missing is a cohesive strategy. You have all these silos and varied opinions and, although all of you are right in the context of your area or silo, things aren't working from the big picture standpoint.

And that leads me to my next slide, which is all about creating a cloud command and control center.

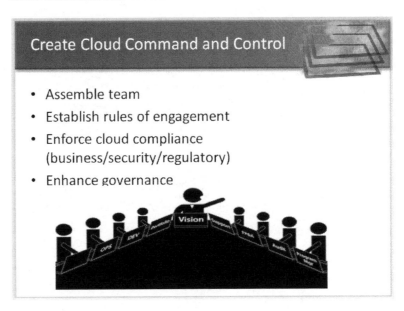

Kayla: For the rest of the morning we are going to work on these areas that you see in the slide, starting with the first essential ingredient of any cloud command and control center, assembling the right team. I'd like you to look around the room. Who's sitting at this table? Is it just the technology architects or developers? Or just the business leadership?

Who else is often not consulted until way into the project or not at all due to silos? Financial planning and analysis for starters. Audit and compliance. Service portfolio managers, also known as product managers. Application engineering and infrastructure engineering. Operations and support. Governance and reporting. All of these roles are essential, but they are often overlooked when the project gets started.

Why is making sure all these areas are represented so important to overall success? Charles, can you take a stab at this one?

Charles: Sure, Kayla. Each and every one of you holds an essential piece that contributes to the larger picture. Just like with a puzzle, if any pieces are missing, the picture is ruined. If we're going to tame the hydra, we're going to have to set aside political and personal agendas and work together. All of us, whether on the business or the technology side of the house, have seen projects that have run over budget and missed expectations in terms of savings and value. In each and every case, poor communication and a lack of cooperation have been at the root of the problem. When communication and cooperation break down, we make decisions and move forward on limited or inaccurate information about what is required from the various roles across the organization.

For the first task, my role is to facilitate communication across the groups represented here. Each of you is here today to fulfill a critical role in this overall program. What we are working on today goes beyond the days you spend in this workshop. As leaders, you must ensure that the rules, regulations and requirements are created, distilled and followed not only from the top down but bottom up.

Look around the table, folks. I have intentionally invited leaders across business and technology to tackle Universal Kingdom's challenges together. Each of you is a member of the Universal Kingdom cloud command and control center. Each of you is accountable for the area of the company you represent, for creating rules and enforcing them with your teams.

Kayla, do you mind if I go ahead and talk about the "rules of engagement" bullet on your slide?

Kayla   Please go right ahead.

Charles   Okay. We have three rules.

The first is about respect. Each of us will respect the fact that we all have different requirements, perspectives, skills and expertise. That is why we're all at the table. So each time we meet, we're going to check politics and agendas at the door.

Rule number two is that everyone has a voice and vote. I expect each member to voice their requirements and weigh in on new policies. So come prepared with knowledge of requirements and market research to share so we can make informed decisions.

> **Rules of engagement:**
>
> - Respect for differences
> - A voice and a vote
> - Reponsibility and accountability

Rule number three, everyone is responsible and accountable. But once the policies are in place, the team will need to accept, enforce and measure the performance of policies we create.

Unless there are any questions about the rules of engagement, I'll turn the floor back over to Kayla.

Kayla: Thank you, Charles. We are well on our way through the first two key objectives. Charles did an excellent job at laying the high-level foundation. However, as a team we also need to establish rules of engagement for lower-level team members and how they will work together.

Although it's critical that this team lead by example, it's just as critical that policies and detailed implementation decisions are driven down to the employee level. For example, one company I worked with would try to decide elements at the executive level. This led to high attrition, low morale and, eventually, unsuccessful implementations.

What are some rules of engagement we can create to empower our employees and ensure that they are following policies established? Rahul?

 Rahul   Well, in keeping the spirit of Charles' general rules of engagement, I'd say that even at lower levels, all roles should be respected for their contributions.

 Suriya   I agree. And then, although everyone should have a voice and a vote, we need a leader at each level to address conflict and bubble up decisions that need to be made by leadership. Also, I think it's important that, while all members of our team weigh in on an area, each area gets to make the final decision for its piece. For example, Rahul should not be dictating to the client operations people what he believes the answer for our role would be. Take the JRE version. We have legacy applications that need different versions. It would be very difficult if new solutions dictated upgrades that would break other applications.

> **Rules of engagement for all:**
>
> - Respect for differences
> - A voice and a vote for all, but a leader at each level to escalate issues
> - Responsibility and accountability
> - Each area owned by the owner of the budget
> - Balance needs of concurrent initiatives

Ben

Agreed. The same would be true for networking or server engineering. There's a lot of convergence right now around cloud and client computing, and it's driving up the costs of network, storage and servers. We need to drive areas that impact our budget. Could we say that each area is owned by the owner of the budget?

 Kayla

Look, both Ben and Suriya are right. But perhaps we could discuss a different approach. What happens for larger implementations that require cross-functional solutions? What you are describing, once again, gets us back to silos. For larger initiatives like cloud computing, the responsibility spans silos. For example, client operations will, to your point, Ben, have an impact on networking and storage for the initiative to move employees from corporate to home offices. What other initiatives are concurrently affecting the same resources and systems?

 Ben:

There are several. That's what makes our role so tough. Let me just list the competing services that are coming online, all with the same target delivery timeframe:

- There's remote workforce, where we're moving employees from company offices to home offices on VDI and Aruba.

- There's the whole BYOD initiative that has increased network traffic and has a huge impact on security audits and risks.

- Our call center is working on an integrated, unified communications solution with our call center application.

- We're creating a cloud call center — migrating our on-premise application to a SaaS solution.

- Then, there's the data center consolidation and optimization project. That includes integrated cloud across a leading cloud provider, public and virtual private cloud, our telephony provider and a backup cloud provider. Plus the creation of an on-premise private cloud.

- We're moving from cloud to managed service with three key providers.

- And, last but not least, we're introducing a new online financial planning application for customers.

Kayla   Ben, what would you say are your biggest challenges in rolling out all these solutions?

Ben   Priority, accountability, process and buy in.

Priority because every one of you guys says your project is the top priority. Not every project can be number one, and there's no way we can implement all these solutions without the risk of destabilizing the entire stack.

As for *accountability*, my costs are skyrocketing as I try to meet these services, but the budget and visibility are just not there. Meaning, some of the savings that my peers are counting on are actually costing us more in ISP, storage and resources to support the higher demand. The leaders in these areas need to be accountable for every aspect of their service and to pay for what they use. Otherwise we risk clogging the pipe connecting all these solutions.

Let's talk *process*. Current processes don't account for including the networking and data center engineering teams. There is a conflict between agile development, stability and how quickly the business can consume the changes. We need a better-defined process and an end to the clash between ITIL and agile.

And *buy in*. We need it from every executive in this room as well as from your customers, both internal and external. When it comes to dealing with conflicting agendas, if the tone is not set at the top and communicated down the chain of command to employees and customers, the lower-level teams will not get on board with it. We're suffering from a lack buy in today, and it's driving shadow IT not just on the part of the business. IT is just as guilty as anyone about shadow IT solutions.

$ Jorg   Wow, Ben, you've got a lot on your plate. But, look, from my perspective, sales and customers should always come first. Let the revenue drive priority and buy in. That will fix the issues you have.

Kayla   Team, do you think it's that simple? What are other thoughts on Ben's list?

Carolyn   Well, I agree revenue should be the top driver, but it isn't that simple. Ben has some great points here. As chief product officer, it's my team's responsibility to balance maintenance with the need for new products we roll out to market. I think we should trust the people we pay to perform these roles to make these decisions. Furthermore, every leader in this room needs to drive those decisions back into the team.

Like Ben said, as long as the leaders in this room haven't bought in, we'll continue to have competing priorities, employees that work around process and limited visibility into who is spending what. We need to work together to get a handle on this. Suriya, you alluded to this as well. My question for the team is why not let the product and service managers drive priority and decisions for each group to balance the service needs against internal?

Suriya   Each team is the expert at their respective area. We shouldn't add another layer in that stack.

Kayla   We need to question some of these assumptions. Can someone tell me why the company has established the role of product or service manager but somehow thinks it's okay to not enable people in this role to perform their jobs?

(Kayla pauses and looks around the room.)

The silence is deafening here. Okay, this is driving us to the third objective: How do we enforce compliance to business, security and regulatory objectives? All this is great conversation. But if the leaders can't agree to define the roles and responsibilities of each area and empower those employees to do their jobs, then what's the point of having those resources? They sure aren't being utilized to the best of their ability.

The first requirement I am hearing to enforce compliance is empowerment of employees to do their jobs. Elizabeth, you've been awfully quiet. Do you want to help identify other elements needed to enforce compliance?

Elizabeth We need to know what we are complying with. For example, you're saying security, regulatory and business compliance. I think we need to understand beyond the high-level terms what that means for Universal Kingdom.

Paul As the CISO, I worry about security and how it affects compliance to business and regulatory objectives. For example, the BYOD and remote workforce initiatives add quite a bit of risk. Even scarier is that many leaders (including people in this room) knowingly authorize employee requests to store critical data in third-party cloud storage systems and to procure non-approved applications from nonapproved cloud providers.

> **CISO security concerns:**
> - Sensitive data at risk on third-party clouds
> - Nonapproved apps may be downloaded from nonapproved providers
> - Execs approve cloud projects without input

And we've even had leaders enter into multimillion dollar contracts without getting the security or governance groups involved. Just this year alone we had to move three SaaS solution providers to on-premise managed service providers and we found at least 300 applications that were approved without the knowledge of my team. All the work and rework costs a lot of money and it affects morale. How do we solve that? Kayla, how do other companies do it?

Kayla The more successful companies I've worked with don't try to end or completely restrict cloud usage. Instead they create policies that guide and contain what people can and can't do. They put up guard rails.

Paul   Can you give us an example?

Kayla   Sure. You can have a policy that says: IT personnel working with regulated data or applications have to work within a private cloud. But if they're working with less-sensitive applications, they can request burst capacity on a third-party public or virtual private cloud. So, basically, you specify what each role and each user can do within the confines of the risks for the company.

And people learn through experience what they can and cannot do in the cloud based on what's in the best interest of the company. I know a few of you here have young children. Think about when they are learning to walk up the stairs. You don't want to stop them from learning, but you do want to put guard rails that establish boundaries to keep them safe while they learn. And if you're constantly hovering over them to make sure they don't use the stairs unless you say it's okay, you won't be able to focus on other more important tasks.

So does anyone have any thoughts on guard rails we can put around the cloud to limit the amount of risk they can introduce? Rahul?

Rahul   From a development perspective we need to be able to get as much burst capacity as we need and as quickly as possible for setting up development, test and troubleshooting environments. Paul and I were talking yesterday about personal information acts, and I think we should make sure we comply with those kinds of mandates by restricting employee access based on roles and what data they have access to.

For my team, one idea that comes to mind is limiting the type of cloud based on development team role and data. We could create three categories: Highly restricted for production, restricted for dev and test environments that may contain personal information and unrestricted for publicly available information like marketing documents or newsletters from program management.

So, then, anything that falls into the highly restricted category would have to be run in the private cloud. Restricted would be able to burst to a virtual private cloud run by a provider that has key attributes such as data encryption at rest and in flight. And then, for unrestricted items, people could use any provider they choose.

$ Jorg   Hold on, Rahul. All that sounded pretty good up until the last one. We also need to think about cost. Meaning, we were 70 percent over budget for storage, networking and usage of cloud services. Teams are working around the system. Many of the costs were hidden in employee expense reports, with managers approving the charges because it was easier to go to cloud providers than it is to go to IT. If we have the capacity in our private cloud, why burst to a third party? Let's think this through.

Rahul   OK. So what do you suggest?

$ Jorg   I'd tighten the reins a bit on the unrestricted category and specify that teams have to pick private cloud first if we have internal capacity. If we don't have capacity, then approve the burst and charge the cost back to the department. No more using corporate cards to expense services from cloud providers. I'm going to remind everybody that we had several hundred virtual machines being charged to corporate credit cards and no one could tell me what they were being used for because the employees had left the company.

Rahul   That makes sense. What else?

$ Jorg   I'd like to see us negotiate rates with the provider ahead of time based on what we think we're likely to use. That way we can get better pricing and select a payment structure that works for us.

Rahul   I like that.

$ Jorg

Measures like these require more planning. I agree with Kayla and Carolyn. Let's let the product and service managers define the service business case and hold people to it. The business cases should be reviewed quarterly by my team, and each leader should be held accountable with respect to budget that is allocated across the board. That way if someone is way over or way under we can adjust.

🏛 Heidi

Jorg, those are all solid points. I'd like to add that, beyond costs, we need some fundamental ground rules to reduce the risk of lawsuits or issues with our customers in terms of compliance with regulations and business directives. The U.S. Patriot Act conflicts with personal information acts in some of the countries where we do business: Japan, Germany, France. Too often we have to enforce changes after the fact because the developers or service managers don't understand the issues beyond the ITIL checklist they have from the audit team. Some key guidelines I'd like to see would help us comply with concerns around FIG Leaf and blind subpoena.

☁ Kayla

Great point, Heidi. But I'm seeing a lot of blank stares around the room, so maybe you can elaborate on what you're talking about.

🏛 Heidi

Sure. So I think pretty much everyone has heard of Edward Snowden, the NSA analyst who highlighted some of the privileges that the Patriot Act affords the U.S. Government. But the Patriot Act is making a lot of businesses and foreign customers uneasy.

Anyway, let me just get to the point. *FIG Leaf* refers to the government practice of going to any third-party provider and monitoring or requesting records — both phone and data — without the explicit knowledge of the company or customer.

> **FIG Leaf:** Government practice of obtaining records from a third-party provider without a company's knowledge.

Blind subpoena is the business equivalent. So if any party decides to sue Universal Kingdom, that

> **Blind subpoena:** Suing party subpoenas a cloud provider to obtain a company's data.

party can subpoena our cloud provider without our knowledge and gain access to our corporate records and information.

Ⓘ Charles   That's scary.

🏛 Heidi   It is, but we can put a few guard rails in place to reduce the risk. Let's take Rahul's *restricted* category. We need to be able to tell our customers in France that their personal information will be housed at a cloud provider in France, not at some multinational provider. That would allow us to comply with French laws.

For FIG Leaf and blind subpoenas, we have to make sure we never host any sensitive company data or unified communications in third-party cloud provider systems. That means anything that could ever be used against us in a lawsuit or create cause for further audits. No matter how we disassemble and reassemble the data, remember that with U.S. Export Commerce Compliance approvals, all the encryption and decryption keys are also submitted to the government.

All data and applications and system solutions have to comply with key compliance directives like Sarbanes Oxley, HIPAA, Graham Leach Bliley, Basel I and II, and other personal information acts.

☁ Kayla   I would also recommend that you add that all applications, data and infrastructure follow the standards created by the NIST guidelines around cloud compliance. The Cloud Security Alliance has also published guidelines. To stay on top of changes in technology that are occurring, the more successful companies will work with the Distributed Management Task Force to help craft the standards that ultimately are used to create the audit standards.

From the themes of the discussion so far, I'm envisioning a chart that graphically depicts and simplifies what everyone is saying here. Let's take a break, and Ben, Carolyn and Muneer, could you spend some time putting a chart together based on our recent exercise for implementing a private cloud? Let's all get back together at 11:00.

(Team reassembles and Kayla pulls up the following chart.)

If			Then
🕐	🔒	$	
↓	—	↓	Public|SaaS
↓	↑	—	Virtual Private
↑	↑	↓	Private + Physical

Time = 🕐   Security = 🔒   Cost = $

Kayla   So, thanks to Ben, Carolyn and Muneer, we now have a chart that sums up the issues and precautions we discussed this morning. They fall into three categories: cost, compliance or security, and time to value.

So how do we use the chart? Well, let's say the business needs a service and time to value is low, or short, meaning it's needed ASAP. Let's say compliance is not a concern and costs are less of a concern for one reason or another. Based on the chart, public cloud or a SaaS solution makes sense. Can someone give me an example of a project that would fall into this area?

Carolyn   The holiday video we do for customers. It has to be out by December 15th to cover all the different holidays our customers celebrate. The final file size is pretty big, and sending it out by email isn't an option. So we have to host it somewhere. And if the data leaks out, there's no real risk to the company. We could create it using an approved public cloud provider and have the provider host it for us.

Kayla   Great. Ben, how about an example that aligns with column 2 in the chart? So, something you need quickly and the compliance risks are high, but cost isn't a big factor.

Ben

Well, given that the risks and time to value are high, the recommendation would be to build out the service on a VPN. We could use a third-party cloud provider on a dedicated environment that connects to our firewall, or we could hire resources to build out an internal private cloud infrastructure. Or we could do both.

This could work for the quarterly analytics we run on customer patterns and usage. We need to protect the data to comply with personal information acts and we need it completed in a timely manner. And regardless of the situation, we make the budget for this exercise based on importance to our reporting to the street. We could use a third-party VPN to perform the burst analytics, do the backup and decommission when it's all done. That approach would minimize costs and risks.

Kayla

Really good example. Muneer, can you give us an example that fits the profile in column 3 on the chart?

 Muneer

This one is a good eye chart. I wish I had it during our migration to private cloud. Okay, so this is a profile of a service where we have more time to implement, security and compliance are big concerns for these systems, and the budget to make changes is limited. My recommendation is private cloud and physical.

I know some of you are thinking, "Why physical?" Well, when we started to review applications to move to our private cloud, we discovered that it didn't make sense to move some of them. The applications were running perfectly well on a small desktop or server with backup. Only a handful of employees were using them. Maybe they were in a small branch office. Or maybe they were going to be replaced six months down the road.

Virtualizing the solution would have been a waste of money and would have created some negative impacts on the network and security. So we opted to leave them on the physical system. Bottom line: We were able to end of life more systems and we didn't have to build out a bigger private cloud infrastructure than we needed.

$ Jorg   Makes sense.

 Muneer   For the critical applications that it made sense to move — things like accounting and mission-critical proprietary applications — it was less expensive and less risky to run them on our internal private cloud. On average, from our analysis and customer references, we found it was about one-third the price of turning it over to a cloud provider.

$ Jorg   Muneer, you really got my attention there. How was it one-third the price? Can you help us understand that one more?

Kayla   Jorg, I assisted Muneer in building out that model. Could we wait until we get to the session on modeling?

$ Jorg   Sure, I can wait.

Kayla   Great. Let's break for lunch. When you come back, please bring the following items with you:

- Any flow charts and information process analysis maps you have — whether they are current or future state — for services, procedures and processes

- A catalog of services you'd like to leverage on the cloud; make sure you have objectives, an executive summary and baseline requirements for each service

- Sample SLAs and service level mapping for services

Food for Thought

What are some actions you can do to create your own workshop to cross the cloud chasm? Follow these simple actions and considerations to recreate Day 1 for your company.

Action	Considerations
Assemble the team	Who will you invite to your table? Why? Remember, don't let politics cloud your judgment or put up obstacles along the road to cloud success.
Assess current state	Do you know what the current state is? Do you have a hybrid hydra and not realize it? Have you educated executives on the pitfalls and risks of failing to tame the hydra? What goals and objectives do you hope to achieve by leveraging cloud in the next 12, 18 and 24 months?
Create rules of engagement	As a group, write down your rules of engagement for approaching cloud. Are they the same as Kayla's? As the Universal Kingdom team's? Why or why not? How would you change, elaborate on or adapt them for your company?
Create cloud positioning system chart	What factors are important for your company? Which are not? Are there factors that have greater impact that are not listed – for example, staff skill sets or maturity? Are there requirements in some areas for multiple levels of security or compliance clearance by government mandates?

Afternoon Session: Create the Roadmap Current to Cloud

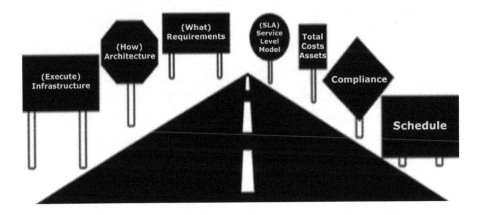

Objectives

Assess current state, identify challenges and risks, create vision and plan (roadmap)

Session Background/Overview

By the end of this session you will understand:

- The four parts of a cohesive roadmap
- Best practices for assessing risk and identifying gaps in people, process and technology
- Risks of shadow IT, consumerization of IT

The Action

(Kayla, with assistance from product management and engineering, leads the team in performing a gap analysis and creating a comprehensive business requirements document (BRD).)

Universal Kingdom Cloud Roadmap

4 Parts of a Cohesive Roadmap

- **What:** Business service requirements
- **When:** Clear timelines/potential delivery schedules
- **Why:** Clear objectives and KPIs
- **How:** Identification of people/process/technologies required to architect a solution

Kayla   Welcome back. I hope you came back refreshed because our subject matter for this afternoon is going to require a lot of brain power. The job at hand is to create a cohesive cloud roadmap. And as the slide up on the screen shows, a cohesive cloud roadmap has four parts:

- Clearly defined business service requirements

- Clearly anticipated timelines and potential delivery schedules

- Clearly defined objectives and key performance indicators

- Identification of the people, process and technology needed to architect a solution

Muneer   Kayla, this sounds similar to the business service management concept.

Kayla   It does, Muneer. BSM, as we discussed earlier, had the best intentions and the right thinking. But what gets missed in many BSM implementations is the last and most critical mile — the business service requirements.

BSM defined what needed to happen from an infrastructure perspective but failed to clearly define the business aspects that drive the services. Remember, each service that IT delivers to business users should fulfill a distinct need that directly benefits the company. The principles may sound familiar, as there have been a few individuals who have applied some of the early principles of BSM that have since been overshadowed by the technology. Carolyn, can you give me an example of how business should drive technology decisions and not the other way around?

Carolyn   My favorite example actually came from working with a large hospital chain in a previous life. The IT people were so excited about the latest updates in technology that they completely overlooked the fact that the hospital was in a major budget crisis because the cost of manufacturing blood was skyrocketing. The CEO wouldn't clear any services that didn't support driving down costs or adhering to compliance requirements. One clever IT administrator built out a brilliant business case on how bringing automation to the manual process for medical billing would reduce overhead and costs and free up more funds to purchase more blood.

At first, the other IT executives whose projects hadn't been approved were upset that this project was funded. When they complained to the CEO, he explained that the hospital is in the business of servicing patients not implementing technology. He made it clear that IT people who want projects approved need to speak the language of the business and justify their projects based on solving business needs.

Kayla   That's an excellent example. I never realized blood was so expensive or that hospitals were considered manufacturers.

	Okay, so to reiterate, IT must speak the language of the business or else the result could be a bloody disaster. Anyone else have an example they'd like to share?

Muneer Sure. The last company I worked for was one of the first to implement BSM. So this definitely feels like *déjà vu*. We learned the hard way that BSM affected many areas of the business. As a result, everyone wanted to own it from an IT perspective and the business didn't understand it. Before we were able to make it work, we had to hire a consultant to build out the business cases. Yes, I mean *cases*, plural. We finally started realizing that we had to understand what we wanted from a business

> What the company expects to get out of the technology dramatically affects the architecture.

perspective before we could do an effective job of building the BSM foundation. The bottom line is that what the company expects to get out of the technology has a huge impact on the architecture.

Kayla So you're saying that a lot of the things you learned from implementing BSM can apply to cloud?

Muneer Absolutely.

Kayla So, given that you and I have worked on this one before, can you elaborate on how BSM correlates to what we have done on the cloud. What was the difference in approach?

Muneer The cloud, like BSM, sets off core debates around ownership, requirements and viability in the route to value.

Kayla That's right. Why do you think that is, Rahul?

Rahul Well, I think in a lot of BSM projects, development teams often believed they should own the configuration management database that was the heart of BSM. The issue is everyone had a different opinion on how to implement it. That led to infighting and a lack of cooperation. And, and in companies that weren't careful, the BSM implementations failed.

A colleague told me that in his company the CMDB changed hands across four VPs. And it wasn't implemented correctly until the CIO stepped in and forced his direct reports to work together for a solution. From our discussions in this workshop, it appears that we are in a similar situation. Everyone thinks they know what's best for implementing the cloud. But I can see a major breakdown in communication across silos. I can also see that we're all trying to do what is best for the company, but each of us comes to the table with a different view and understanding of what cloud computing is.

Kayla   Why do you think that is? What is the most challenging part about creating a cohesive strategy?

Rahul   I'd say a lack of visibility that's preventing us from knowing where to start. In fact, ironically, it really centers around the CMDB. Kayla, the problem is that a lot of the data is housed in multiple CMDBs that aren't integrated. So there's no visibility across them. We desperately need visibility into usage, but it isn't available to balance licenses and usage and to determine how we're performing against the KPIs that are important to the business.

Kayla   Why not start where you are?

Rahul   Not sure what you mean by that?

Carolyn   Perhaps Rahul needs a cloud positioning system — like the global positioning system in his car. That way he can figure out where he is.

Jorg   That's a good one, Carolyn. And while we all got a chuckle out of it, the reality is that we are tasked with creating that very thing for the company. If you guys don't know where you are, how can you figure out where you need to be? You may get to your destination eventually, but that will be one long, expensive trip.

Muneer   Yes, Jorg, the devil is in the details, and we better know our details or we'll have a better chance of going to Hades than getting funding for our cloud effort.

Kayla   Knowing where you are is critical. Before you can come up with a cohesive strategy you have to have certain things in place. It's just like when you're getting ready to bake a cake. You need to know what kind you're going to bake. Is it a chocolate cake or a cheesecake? If you don't know the desired outcome, how do you ensure you have the right ingredients, tools and skills to start?

Heidi   Good thing we're not in the bakery business or we would be out of business from the blank stares around the room.

Kayla   Okay, let's map out a current state by answering some fundamental questions about where we are. And I just happen to have a slide on that.

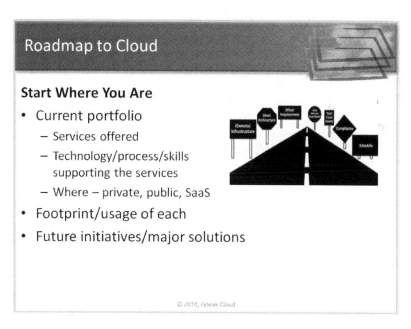

Kayla   Take a look and, honestly, you may be pleasantly surprised that you have more answers than you think. Figuring out your current state isn't that difficult, and it definitely doesn't require two months or a black belt in Six Sigma process mapping. What it does require is documenting some fundamental pieces.

Ben, Muneer, what tools do you use to determine how many servers you need? Or how do you know if you are meeting your service level agreements?

 Ben

That's easy. My team creates the tools we need for operations. We have a CMDB that contains overviews of installations and where the assets are located. We have monitoring tools — both vendor provided and custom open source — that tell us the health of the service, and we have other tools that provide aggregated dashboards on overall usage and utilization of network, hardware and storage.

Kayla

Great. That's what I was hoping to hear. Now, how do you tie that back to your cloud implementation?

Ben

We don't exactly. The cloud infrastructure is only partially in the CMDB and when we lift and shift workloads, it throws our assessment off. And, I hate to say it, but not all tools are using our inventory or CMDB capabilities. Only a handful of the custom-built applications leverage what we built for the dashboards.

Kayla

Muneer, what do you use for your cloud solutions?

Muneer

That's complicated. The gap is that many of the solutions were built for static, on-premise applications. They don't do a good job of handling the dynamic nature of private, public or SaaS clouds. In fact, I was just speaking with my buddy, Ben Gordon from R3P software. He mentioned that there is still a gap between the solutions. So, essentially, we have different solutions depending on the technology, what APIs are available to integrate them and where they are located. For public cloud providers, we only need to monitor the software layer of the stack. That limits what we need and can collect. Our private cloud needs to monitor both hardware and software, but at the speed of lifting and shifting.

Rahul

That's great information, Muneer, but will you answer the question? What are you using for cloud solutions?

Muneer	A combination of homegrown monitoring that extends one in-house solution and one open source tool. We leverage a data aggregation tool to create dashboards for visibility on various services. To my point above, when a service uses multiple solutions located on different layers in the cloud stack, monitoring it accurately becomes a challenge.
Kayla	Okay, how do you tie your legacy components of the service back to the cloud?
Carolyn	Fairy dust? Perhaps a bit of magic? Seriously, it sounds like we don't tie it back, which from a business perspective is a bit scary.
Muneer	No this is not a princess movie and we don't have fairy godmothers waiting in our server room. We write custom dashboards that pool from various locations.
Rahul	Perhaps we could use a fairy godmother in the data center because the current method breaks our processes for change management and inventory management, and limits visibility of the service.
Kayla	Let's stop with the fairytales and get down to brass tacks, shall we?
All	Sure.
Kayla	Part of "starting where you" is assessing what's in place in terms of people, process and technology. From the little exchange that just took place, I've gleaned the following:

- One: Current service management processes are not being followed for the cloud, so the company is struggling with bifurcated processes.
- Two: You've got multiple tools but no single system of record to set as master.
- Three: The data center team has skills in coding, merging data records and creating dashboards that could be customized if off-the-shelf tools will not work.
- Four: Services do not appear to be well defined.

- And five: There are mixed emotions about the success of the current operation, the quality of the data from it and how intensive it is to maintain.

Anyone want to add anything to my assessment?

Carolyn I'd just say that number four is accurate to a point. We really try to define the services, but they keep changing.

Heidi The only guarantees in life are change, death and taxes. Seriously, we can't just say, "Sorry, we can't cope with change." With all the new regulations and industry changes, we have to be able to adapt in a heartbeat.

Kayla Heidi raises an excellent point. Carolyn, what templates do you use for defining the baseline of the services you offer to your customers?

Carolyn We are an agile shop.

Kayla That is great but what template do you use to define the nonstory requirements?

Carolyn Not sure what you mean. As I said, we're an agile shop. We write user stories and the development and operations teams implement them. Note that we try to keep them in the business capability mode to ensure that they are high level enough for a conversation but not restrict things with too much detail.

Kayla I see. But, listen, a lot of IT shops I've worked with claim to be agile, but when you dig under the covers they are not really agile, and they are not waterfall. I've seen a lot of cases where people create a pseudo process to be somewhere in between because of the nature of the task they are trying to accomplish. For example, setting up and configuring

> **Runbook:**
>
> Spells out the order in which configuration steps need to occur.

hardware usually requires distinct steps and understanding what the runbook is. Some people call the runbook a configuration sequence or configuration template, but it's basically the order in which the configuration has to happen.

Carolyn   But what about our goals for agile development?

Kayla   Agile is great. But it doesn't work for everything. If you have a hardware setup, you can't just set it up as requirements come in. You need a runbook process so that things happen in the right order. Waterfall, or maybe keychaining is a better word. That's what you need. Here's an example: If you're setting up database, web and app servers to support an IT service, you need to install the database server and its schema before you can set up the app server. Otherwise the app server doesn't have any place to deposit data. And you have to get the web server set up before the app server because the application won't run without the web server.

Ben   Finally someone other than Ops gets it. Every time I hear we need to be more agile or that we are implementing DevOps, it makes the hair on the back of my neck stand up. And the same is true of people saying that things are cheaper just because they are in a cloud. It just isn't always true.

Rahul   Here we go. Look, Ben, DevOps and creating continuous deployment is critical for our ongoing success. We have to be flexible and agile enough to address critical business needs and to maintain compliance.

Kayla   There is a middle road here. When you're driving a car, there are basic guidelines — rules that we all need to understand before we get behind the wheel. But how we drive, what routes we take and how frequently we stop varies depending on the journey and the destination. Moving to cloud is not any different if you think about it. Before you set off on a trip, you need to ensure you have a good estimate of what it will take in terms of people, process and technology, what the service levels will be, and what success looks like. How many of you have heard of RASSSS?

ⓘ Charles   RASSSS interesting word. Where does it come from?

☁ Kayla   I just happen to have a slide.

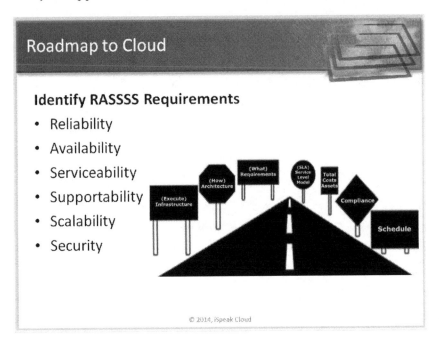

RASSSS is an acronym I strongly encourage you to use to define the nonagile requirements. It covers reliability, availability, serviceability, supportability, scalability and security. Let's go through each one:

- How **reliable** does the system need to be? What are the expectations in terms of service load and requirements to maintain the system?
- Then we have **availability.** What's the required uptime? Availability needs vary with the service. For example, our website has a 99.9 percent availability while the accounting application has a 25 percent availability, as it is needed for only part of the year.
- Next is **serviceability**. What will the service model need to be to actually support the application or service? How many

anticipated patch updates will there be? What is the defined frequency? Think "Microsoft Patch Tuesday." This is all about setting expectations on when an update will happen or not.

- Then we have **supportability**. What's the support model for the service? Will you have tier 1 (help desk), tier 2 (advanced troubleshooting) and tier 3 (development level) support? Or is the product mature enough for a partial tier 1 call and resolution by development as needed?

- What are the **scalability** requirements in terms of the number of users? You need this information to determine load testing, network usage and other elements based on similar applications. Scalability is often an overlooked but critical aspect of any cloud model.

- And, finally, what **security** and regulatory rules apply. The cloud model you choose has a huge impact on security. For example, regulations for public cloud are much more stringent than for private. It's vital to know the security requirements in advance so you can architect them into the solution. Studies show that once you're in production, it can cost 100 times more to address a missing requirement than it would have cost if you included it in the original design.

Andrew   Can I interrupt for a sec?

Kayla   Sure.

Andrew   I want to emphasize how important security is, and I really appreciate that the business realizes we need to think about security and compliance earlier rather than later so we can be thorough about assessing risks. One thing we're running into is that many of these architectures we're dealing with were put into place before a lot of these regulations came into being. How do we keep up? How do we architect for change not only in technology but also in security and compliance as laws change and new regulations are issued?

Heidi   Anyone have a crystal ball so we can look into the future to answer Andrew's question?

Kayla
I'm no fortune teller, but there are safeguards you can put into place to adhere to regulations. Let's face it, there are more regulations now than ever before due to the global dependency on technology in more and more areas. Keeping up is an insurmountable task if you try to track legislation and regulations individually.

Fortunately, a lot of mandates are similar, and their requirements often can apply across solutions. We might also find adjacent industries that are already affected by legislation. We might be able to leverage best

> **Coping with regulatory change:**
> - Look for similarities in requirements
> - Leverage best practices from other industries
> - Leverage current thinking from standards bodies

practices developed by companies in those industries. For example, think about the personal information acts. Graham Leach Bliley affects financial services, while the Health Insurance Portability and Accountability Act applies to healthcare. They are different acts for different purposes, but protecting personal information is pretty much the same across the board.

Rahul
Kayla, what can we do from a development perspective to avoid re-engineering our code every time a new law comes out?

Kayla
Before you come up with solutions, understand what the current thinking is and look to see what may be coming down the pipeline. For example, NIST has released defined standards for audit with cloud computing. Are you internalizing the lists with development or at least architecture to ensure you are building to those standards?

Rahul
We are now.

Andrew
This is great. I feel like we are finally getting somewhere. It isn't that the audit team doesn't want to help. We are just holding people accountable to the standards. We can't tell you what we are looking

for, but if you are following key standards that you can point to, it would make everyone's job a lot easier.

⊙ Charles   I cannot stress enough that I expect everyone to be proactive about compliance whether it is regulatory, security or business directives. Who can take point on ensuring this is implemented? Rahul and Andrew, is this something you can partner on?

🔍 Andrew   Sure, sounds good, right, Rahul?

✺ Rahul   Absolutely.

☁ Kayla   Whether you meant to do it or not, you've moved into the next topic I want to cover — risk assessment. So let me just move on to that slide.

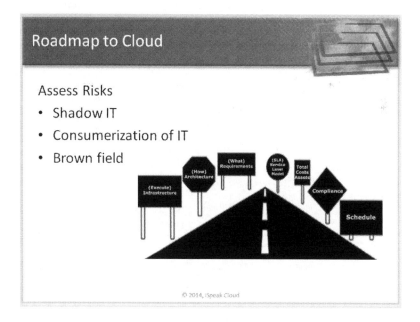

☁ Kayla   Risk assessment often ends up being the 800-pound gorilla in the room that nobody paid attention to and that, in the end, disrupts all kinds of things, from your business model and selection of provider to your architecture. Part of that overall assessment of current state is understanding risks in your current implementations.

And, look, many of the companies I've worked with are in the same boat. They have unintentionally put the cart before the horse and have been implementing solutions in silos. The result is they have increased risk.

What else can the process of performing this risk assessment do for a company? Andrew, want to take this one? It appears to be the one topic that brings you to life.

Andrew   We identify the broken processes and the pockets of shadow IT that people have created to work around them. You know, not long ago, we discovered our call center director had hired some so-called business analysts. In reality, they were developers who were creating their own applications to use in lieu of what IT had created.

The applications were running on third-party clouds and everything was built outside the firewall. Needless to say, we had to shut everything down due to compliance risks. In fact, confidentially, in addition to larger projects like this one, we discovered literally hundreds of smaller ones where individual developers, business leaders or operations staff were using cloud solutions that were not authorized and not secure, or that didn't fit the specifications we needed for compliance.

Jorg   Blatant waste is what this is. Seriously, how much do we think we actually spend in terms of man hours on these shadow processes while trying to maintain broken ones in parallel? I believe that needs more investigation and is a good candidate for cleaning house. Carolyn and Andrew, I want you to take point here.

Carolyn   We'll get right on it.

Kayla   Okay. Let's move on to gap analysis.

Gap Analysis: Current Versus Desired

- Current service and process mappings
- Changes required to reach desired state
- Deltas/changes needed to determine current versus desired state
- Resources impacted
- Gaps in skills, process, or technology to be filled

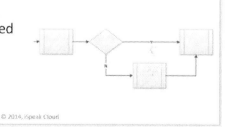

Kayla — Like a global positioning system, you cannot create the cloud positioning system Carolyn mentioned earlier without understanding the landscape, routes to value and what resources you have. Now that we've mapped out the current versus the desired state, we can start identifying the gaps in people, process and technology. Charles, tell us why this is important.

Charles — Simply stated, it's like going shopping for groceries without checking your refrigerator first. How do you know what you need if you don't know what you already have and what's usable or not usable.

Kayla — It must be close to lunch time. That's a great analogy, Charles. You are absolutely right. Many companies have process maps to the nth degree. We can learn a lot from those efforts. Suriya, what can we learn from process maps?

Suriya — Even though some are outdated, what we can tell quickly is whether or not people are actually following the defined processes for a service. It's important to have the end users participate in the conversation. Vision and reality aren't always the same thing, so when the processes hit the call center floor, some work, some don't. The processes that don't function well typically end up in shadow processes or shadow IT. For example, Cobry's group created a spreadsheet to work around the lead-routing application in the call center and manually assign new leads to brokers on the floor. We recently discovered this in a field trip. Ironically, engineering was bragging about the low volume of calls into the service desk for the application. You can imagine how they felt when they found out that there were no calls because no one was using the application.

$ Jorg   What a waste. Not only are we not tracking the time spent developing the VB script spreadsheet, we're also wasting the time our engineering team spends working on the application.

Kayla   Great point. What are other critical factors that go into determining your roadmap? Carolyn?

Carolyn   Once we identify the desired state and current state in terms of requirements, we need to perform an overall gap analysis to determine how far our vision is from reality. I'm talking about things like skill sets, available technology, custom solutions needed, and integrations and processes to be developed for the service to be successful.

Kayla   Again, all great points. Let's talk about the basics of performing a gap analysis prior to mapping out our cloud journey. We've been discussing examples of where shadow IT and processes need to be evaluated to determine the best route to value. As this slide shows, there are three primary areas I typically have my clients focus on when they are performing a gap analysis.

Gap Analysis: Map Journey to Value

Skills, Scope, Strategy

- Skills you have today
- New skills required
- Scope required from a high level for each release

If you don't know enough about requirements to plan at least 2 major and 2 minor releases out, you're not ready.

First is mapping the journey in terms of value, scope and skills. That means figuring out what skills you have and which ones you need to achieve minimal value according to the business case. Although some of these projects can take years to implement, the key is understanding enough about the scope for at least two major and two minor releases in terms of high-level needs to establish a foundation for success.

Second is architecting a solution for the smaller incremental milestone with the larger picture in scope. In other words, start architecting a private cloud solution with the idea that you may have to find a way to integrate into a larger hybrid cloud strategy. This approach is critical because most companies are brownfields with lots of applications and solutions already in place, so integration will be a must. What's more, IT environments are dynamic, so over the course of your project, other projects will be rolling out. Those projects are likely to affect your planning.

Third, always start with a solid business case. Before you decide what the best route is for your company, you've got to understand the true costs and benefits. This ties back to what we discussed earlier about the agile percentages that you can apply and extrapolate forward. If you have a sound business case before deciding to use private cloud, public cloud or a hybrid solution, you will have an idea on what the true cost will be versus benefit to the business. Remember, every business case should highlight KPIs to ensure that the case and its assumptions are still valid. Companies are organic and constantly changing, so the business case needs to be adaptable.

Kayla   Can you give me a brief example from a project or service you are working on today?

Rahul   I have a good example.

Carolyn   She did say brief, Rahul. This isn't going to be another dissertation on DevOps is it?

Rahul   My PhD was not on DevOps, but … point well taken. I will try to keep it brief and be a little less defensive than I was in my presentation on DevOps. The example I was thinking about is around document management service. We are rolling out a new application for portfolio investing for our customers. It leverages a new electronic document management SaaS solution along with our internal legacy applications. We had to pick the best solution that would work with our existing legacy applications, desired business requirements and resource skill sets. In the end, we realized we couldn't select the most feature-rich solution because the adoption costs would be far greater than the benefit.

Muneer   That is a great example, Rahul.

Rahul   I know. So give us the dirt on the project.

Muneer   Well, it really became contentious because a few of the business leaders really wanted the solution with all the bells and whistles. The challenges that came up during the pilot really centered on integrating our existing systems, third-party providers and our infrastructure monitoring tools. The tool they wanted was a bit older and based on proprietary technology. It didn't have the APIs that would enable us to determine the root cause of any application issues. For example, there was no clear way to integrate it to our existing monitoring tools to determine if the service was up or down, or if it was meeting our SLAs with our customers.

Rahul   It looked fancy but really lacked what we needed beyond the bells and whistles. The product we selected didn't have as many features, but had far more open APIs plus easy integration with current tools. The implementation costs were about one-third that of the feature-rich solution because it leveraged more advanced virtualization technologies to reduce the footprint and number of servers required.

Training was also a big factor. The solution was built off of a proprietary technology and would have required retraining our entire development staff on the new language. We were looking at about $500,000 to ramp up employees on the new technology and another $1.5 million in professional services to architect and implement the solution while our team was coming up to speed.

Kayla   This reminds me of another customer I worked with. A large bank replaced its configuration management tool to save money on maintenance. The maintenance had been costing $1 million per year and the new product promised to be only $250,000 per year. On the surface it looked great but after making the decision to move, they quickly realized it was going to take $4 million more a year in operational costs to save the $1 million in maintenance costs due to factors such as a skills shortage, increased footprint that equated to higher operations costs and the cost of training employees on the new systems. So, basically, reducing maintenance costs of a given tool without realizing that the costs would simply shift to another area doesn't necessarily save you any money.

Carolyn   Another point to make here is that you need to understand the requirements to determine the best way to create both a long-term and short-term strategy. Meaning, sometimes you have to replace technology that is going to be obsolete, but if you can do it gradually, you can reduce disruption to the company. Windows XP is a great example. Many companies have been gradually migrating off of XP until it was necessary to replace due to the costs. It turned out in many cases to be less expensive to keep XP than to replace it with workaround solutions that had poorer performance. The key is balancing all the factors in the business case around delivering the service — operations, capital investment and resources.

Kayla   Carolyn, thank you for adding in the last piece. It actually will be part of our homework for tomorrow.

(Kayla passes out a business requirements document template with a sample master planning worksheet to the group.)

I'm giving you all a little light bedtime reading for this evening. It's a sample of a business requirements document template for iterative agile and an accompanying master planning spreadsheet to tie the themes and requirements back to resources for your service planning exercise. Perhaps you have a different method that you would like to incorporate into the final templates.

I'd like each of you bring in examples of how you tie your business requirements back to your processes and gap analysis. For the first half of tomorrow we will review the templates and discuss how they would tie into a business case for cloud.

Have fun. See you in the morning.

> See Appendix A for the template and Appendix B for the worksheet.

Food For Thought

Action	Considerations
Assess current state of service portfolio	Now that you've identified your state of cloud readiness, can you identify the state of your service portfolio readiness? Are your services clearly defined? Do you understand their goals, objectives and KPIs? How will they impact your cloud vision and strategy?
Identify risks	What business or services is IT offering employees and/or customers? Are there inherent risks due to adoption of SaaS solutions or shadow IT?
Create vision and roadmap	As a group, create a sample BRD and master planning sheet, and tie it back to your cloud strategy. Remember to select a smaller project with integration points. Can you see how the interdependencies in people, processes and technology can impact your cloud strategy? What approach did you use for hardware, new products or maintenance?
Tie it into your cloud positioning system chart	Does the chart change based on what you discovered with the service roadmap? Were you able to create a roadmap that ties services to supporting operational infrastructure (internal or external)? Can you see patterns that could work for your company when tying multiple service portfolios to your cloud strategy?

Cloud Quest Workshop Day 2:

Morning Session: Creating a BRD

Objective
Create a baseline roadmap from vision and comprehensive gap analysis.

Session Background/Overview
By the end of this session you will understand:

- Best practices and guidelines for creating an agile-based BRD and master planning template for your cloud strategy
- The difference between various development approaches and how to apply them at various stages in the lifecycle
- How to phase in a successful DevOps strategy with a cloud implementation (the two can coexist harmoniously)
- How cloud and SaaS affect your business case and how to create an accurate case for your cloud strategy

The Action
(Kayla, with assistance from product management and engineering, leads the team in understanding various development methodologies, applying them to creating a cloud strategy and creating a comprehensive business requirements document.)

Gap Analysis: Templates and Tools

Business Requirements Document
- Creates common understanding between business and technology
- Enables communication across stakeholders
  - Addresses business, technology and legal teams
  - Provides a common language/understanding across teams

© 2014, iSpeak Cloud

Kayla — Good morning. Did you all get through your homework? Who wants to start the discussion of the templates and how they relate to the work we were doing yesterday?

Muneer — I really liked the way the templates tied together some of the fundamentals you mentioned yesterday such as RASSSS.

Carolyn — Me too. The things we did yesterday — starting our journey with where we are now, adding in RASSSS, looking at risks and doing the gap analysis — everything feeds into this business requirements document.

Rahul — Kayla, this is all fine and good in terms of discussion. But isn't it a waste of time? We are an agile development shop. BRDs and massive documentation sound like waterfall to me. That type of development methodology is slow and will not meet the growing needs of our business.

Kayla — Rahul, I understand your concern. Other VPs of engineering I have worked with have had that same initial reaction. The business requirements template I handed out yesterday is based on an *iterative agile* approach.

(Kayla points to a diagram she has drawn on a flip chart.)

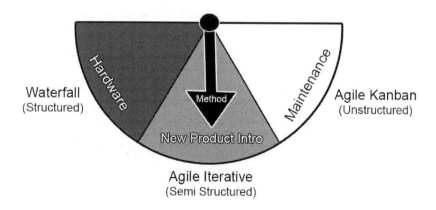

Kayla   Take a look at this diagram. Can anyone tell me what iterative agile is? So, Carolyn, you've been in product management for a number of years. Would you explain what iterative agile is?

Carolyn   I'd say it combines the just-in-time elements of agile development with enough foresight into future development needs to create a 12 to 18 month timeline and breakeven calculations.

Kayla   Not bad. The key to what Carolyn is saying is that it's a hybrid approach. The waterfall BRDs of the past were very detailed, with 50 to 100 pages. An iterative agile BRD should not be more than 25 pages. It provides a baseline synopsis of the requirements and intended solutions without painting a precise picture. Think of it like a blueprint for a house. If you look at the example I provided and the examples your peers brought in, you'll notice some fundamental differences. Who wants to explain how the three approaches differ from each other?

Carolyn   The waterfall example spells out every requirement down to the minute details, and it's all spelled out before development starts. Often with this approach, the developers and business people find that their needs change during the lengthy process.

The Kanban style falls short in that the charter doesn't typically define critical path requirements that aren't actual features — like the ones we talked about yesterday: reliability, availability, serviceability, supportability, scalability and security.

Iterative agile falls in the middle between waterfall and Kanban. There is still some documentation, but only enough to help people understand the foundation and cost implications. It's not so much detail that it inhibits collaboration, cuts out user feedback or prevents developers from delivering value increments in short time frames.

Kayla   Great explanation. Who wants to describe how the BRD templates for the iterative agile approach differ from either pure Kanban-style agile and from waterfall?

Muneer   From what I can see, the iterative agile approach defines at least two major and two minor releases at a high level, but it's detailed enough to determine costs, approximate payloads and timelines. So, using Kayla's analogy of a blueprint for a house, it would spell out that you're building a four-bedroom, two-bath, single-story, 3800 square foot home.

The **BRD** would provide enough information to lay a solid foundation and put in the plumbing, electrical and other key elements, so you can calculate approximate costs. The final details such as specifics on the type of flooring, the cabinets and countertops and other aspects are defined closer to completion as part of the user stories.

The **master planning template** ties in velocity in hours of resource time and interdependent resources to avoid stretching our staff too thin and high-level capabilities to lower-level features as they evolve throughout the development cycle.

Kayla   Muneer, that is correct. What I'm showing you is an example of a master planning template in Microsoft Excel.

#	Business Requirement	Value/$	Scale/ Priority	Actual Release	Target Release	Portfolio
1	High level business benefit to be delivered by a given service or portfolio of services	High	1	V1	1.8	Product Portfolio A (CRM)
2	Business will be able to view account inquiry history	High	1	V3	1.8	Product Portfolio A
3	Business will be able to transfer leads from inside sales reps in legacy systems to new system	Med	1	V2	1.8	Product Portfolio A
4	Business will be able to identify & prioritize work for inside sales reps	High	1	V4	V3 (V2+)	Product Portfolio A/B

There are a few software solutions in the market that try to provide this capability. The key, as you point out, is that it stitches together multiple business requirements across multiple initiatives across resources, time to value and priority. Think back to the slide on elements of a roadmap. The master planning tool helps to stitch them all together, focusing on measuring the why, what, who, when and what it costs.

Gap Analysis: Templates and Tools

Master Planning Spreadsheet
- Ties high-level requirements to resources/timelines
- Facilitates communication
    - Projected timelines for completing each project phase
    - Resource requirements, velocity, interdependencies
    - Priority and high-level delivery scope of requirements

© 2014, iSpeak Cloud

Charles What are critical elements we should look for in the master planning tool or template?

Kayla Whether you select an off-the-shelf tool or create a master template, the critical elements are the same.

Master Planning Template:

What:

- Initiatives, programs and subprojects to be delivered and what has to be timed together or needs to be avoided to reduce bottlenecks

- Prioritized in descending order based on supported business value (both monetary and intrinsic)

The "what" is the master list based on value to the business and executive priority presented in a clear hierarchy of the service initiatives, programs and applications breakdown. More complicated services, such as CRM, have a larger hierarchy with more initiatives, programs and projects that are nested under one another. There are also smaller services such as email. Remember, this should be broken down by priority and subpriority of each service component based on time to value and business benefit to the company. All the business capabilities and underlying user stories should be prioritized based on their value to the service business case.

Who:

- Resources required to deliver services broken down by role, skill sets, and velocity in hours

FTE	Team	Time	Group	Count Dev	Count
Dev					
Architect 1	SaaS	0.5	CRM		0.5
Architect 1	SaaS	0.5	Unified Comm		0.5
Architect 2	SFDC	0	Unified Comm		0.5
Architect 2	SFDC	0	CRM		0.5
Developer	SFDC		CRM		1
Developer		50	CRM		0.5
System Admin 1	SFDC	50	CRM		0.5
System Admin 2		50	CRM		0.5
System Admin 3	SFDC	50	CRM		0.5

The "who" is about your resources and a measurement of their velocity to accomplish a set task. This is critical for shared resources that tend to be the bottlenecks — databases, networking and security. A successful implementation requires tightly managing the swim lanes and reducing hot spots and cold spots across your resource pool.

When:

Time to value — when each payload will bring the biggest value. Add targets — what sprints, what weeks or timelines to target delivery, and velocity of team. *Contributes to calculating and forecast costs.

Release	FY 14 - Q1			FY 14 - Q2	
	Jan	Feb	March	April	May
Week 1					
Week 2	1	1	1	1	1
Week 3					
Week 4	1	1	1	1	1
Week 5	0.5				0.5
	DevOM	QAOM	MDWOM	DevCM	QACM
V 1.0					
V 1.5	200	100		#REF!	#REF!
V 1.8	70	70		1382	2247
V2				728	1666
V2.0 Data					
V 3.0 All In					
Total Hrs wee	330				
	120				

The **"when" relates to timelines.** You'll need the ability to manage timelines visually based on targeted windows of time to value from the business case. For example, how many sprints overall does the project need to deliver the first payload? The second? The third? Are there any blackout windows due to business or technology constraints that need to be considered and communicated?

Master Planning Template:

Costs:

Breakdown of capital expenses (CapEx) and non-capital expenses also known as operational expenses (OpEx).

Initiative	Capitalized?	Q1 2014	Q2 2014	Q3 2014	Q4 2014
CRM Licenses - SaaS	No	1,500,000	1,500,000	1,500,000	1,500,000
CRM Contractor Expenses for Customization	No	875,000	875,000	875,000	875,000
On Prem Product A (Email)	Yes	300,000	300,000	300,000	300,000
On Prem Product A (Email Maintenance)	No	45,000	45,000	45,000	45,000
Company XI Unified Communications System	Yes	600,000	600,000	600,000	600,000
Company XI Unified Communications System Maintenance	No	90,000	90,000	90,000	90,000

Finally, the "cost visualization." Few out-of-the-box tools have this component, but I have seen customers create custom dashboards that integrate service components — technical resources — with service labor resources to visually burn down to adjust time to value and identify breakeven points.

Rahul I like the user story example and how the stories tie back to the master planning spreadsheet. One area where we always find contention is database administration. This method looks like it will allow us to plan at least one quarter out and move items in or out to reduce bottlenecks. I'm starting to see how it still follows agile but gives us some much-needed structure.

(Rahul points to user story Excel sheet.)

A	B	C	D	E	F
Author	1=Critical, 2=High, 3=Med, 4=Low	Business Capability	Product	Epic (feature)	"(User or system) should be able to _____ so that they can _____"
Marissa Sato	1	Electronic Statements	Online Banking	Historical Search	The Online Banking system is to display icons representing each statement for the last 12 month period to the user when the statement feature is clicked.

G	H	I	J	K	L	M	N
Detailed Description (sub requirements)	Acceptance Criteria	ns (What must be in place for feature/function to be valuable?)	Comments / Questions [name]	Exists today	Roadmap	Time To Value	Product Mgr
Additional statements past 12 months should have a more statements button	When the user clicks on the statement search button icons with the date for each statement will appear on the screen	Adobe PDF Reader, Search cabaility	Service level agreement of 98.9%	N	Y	9/1/13	Carolyn Zarate

Kayla   Great! Glad to see you're evolving your thinking. Note from my diagram on the board that there is a time and place for each method. Operations will always prefer waterfall because typically hardware and base application installs require a process or steps to follow. Development will typically favor the Kanban style of agile because it reduces the time required to address changes and critical issues for mature products. The business and product groups may take a more pragmatic approach, however, for new product introduction with iterative agile. The blueprint example earlier illustrates why iterative agile is so important in these cases. It gives managers and senior leaders enough visibility into timing and costs that they can manage the change and financial aspects of the service lifecycle.

Charles   All this sounds great in theory. But how do you manage costs and timelines realistically? This is an area we've really struggled with.

Kayla   Many companies do struggle with this. There are known models that provide a realistic ballpark. From my experience, an iterative agile model follows a formula — 25 percent of capacity for new features, 25 percent for hardening, 30 percent for agile unknowns and 20 percent pad for holidays. Adding the 30 percent still provides the burn down that is typically found in agile but also provides structure based on capacity to determine overall costs. It's built into the example for master planning and overall business case.

Rahul   How does all this fit into cloud computing? Forgive me but I am trying to connect the dots here.

Kayla   If you remember our discussions yesterday, we needed to define the what, why, when and how to understand the best routes to cloud value. The real value in implementing the right size and type of cloud components for your company depends on the services you are offering and the value or overall costs. At the end of the day, companies need to focus on their business results and the route to value may vary depending on the company and its services and needs.

The introduction this afternoon on building the business case will provide some clarity in these areas to balance the costs, time to value and approach.

Calculating Costs – Service to Cloud

Business Case 101

- Cash flow model versus profit and loss

- Capital expense (CapEx) vs operational expense (OpEx)

- Impact of cloud on business case

© 2014, iSpeak Cloud

Kayla   Okay, I hope everyone is ready to be stretched to the limit.

Rahul   Looks like this next part of the workshop entails a lot of math.

Kayla   It does, but what's important is not knowing math but understanding how the different processes and formulas can make a difference in determining actual costs versus the picture painted of not only your cloud environment but also the services you are supporting.

Charles   I want everyone to make sure your cell phones are turned off, email is shut down and you're really paying attention. Last year we were off by nearly 40 percent on our budgets. We overstated business benefits across programs and projects for cloud by 55 percent, and had to make some pretty extensive cuts to bring things back into alignment. As an organization, we're really dependent on technology, and we know the right technology can be a huge driver of success. But we need to figure out how we refine, align and create a more effective strategy so that we can actually achieve our overarching objectives. At the end of the day, it's all about dollars and cents. Jorg, is there anything you would add?

$ Jorg   Well, I'd say that one of the key concerns is that the enhanced systems that are supposed to be saving money aren't. As a company we need better visibility into costs and we need people to manage to budgets. Ideally, after this workshop, we'll have a better breakdown to understand true total cost of ownership. All of this agile speak sounds great when it comes to delivering something for the business. The problem is it's really difficult for us to cost out and get our arms around.

Carolyn   Jorg, I'm confused. We work closely with financial planning and analysis to create the business cases that we have in place for investment. What's the issue?

$ Jorg   It's hard to put my finger on it. If I knew all the root causes, we'd have already addressed them and we wouldn't be here.

Cobry   Perhaps if the product people aren't sure about their costing models, we should default to the business leads for those areas. I completely understand the costs of my team and what we need. Why are we forced to do shadow IT, as you call it?

$ Jorg   Cobry, are you sure about that? It was your team that ran up the majority of the unauthorized costs with Amazon. My team has identified tens of thousands that are being charged to corporate cards that are not part of any budget. What you're overlooking is the costs for my people to hunt through all the expense reports to determine what is technology spend versus business spend. We have had to restate quite a bit where the budget was off.

Cobry   We can talk about that one offline, Jorg. I'm still not convinced that those costs are correct. I've run the numbers and mine don't match up with what finance has indicated in our quarterly true up.

Kayla   It's great to see such enthusiasm for this topic. It's a tough one as we can see already. To Jorg's point, if the numbers were adding up, you wouldn't need this workshop. Let's try to dig into why everyone is correct and everyone is off. Carolyn, what type of business modeling does your team perform for creating a service-to-cloud strategy?

Carolyn   We use a basic cost and benefit business case model. I'm not sure why our model would be in question here. We've been using it for the entire decade I've been with Universal Kingdom. It works.

Kayla   Carolyn, it's not about right or wrong. What we are talking about, though, is perhaps shifting the model a bit. Jorg, what models do you use in accounting and financial planning and analysis?

Jorg   We use standard cash flow and profit and loss models. Why?

Kayla   Can you explain to the group how those two models differ from each other? Noting that, although many executives are familiar with the various model names, it's nice to have a simple refresher that people can take back to their teams.

Jorg   Cash flow models are simple models that look at overall cash inflows and outflows for a given period. Companies with more cash on hand are more

> http://www.investopedia.com/terms/c/cashflow.asp

solvent. They can pay their bills and invest more than companies that have everything invested in capital assets. There's a website called investopedia that has details. I'll write the link here on the flipchart. If you want more details or you want your direct reports to learn more, you can suggest they go to this site. P&L models take it a step further in that they factor in additional expenses and benefits, such as depreciation for capital expenditures, in determining the overall profitability or loss.

Kayla   Jorg, great explanation. Now, Muneer, can you tell us why different models can generate drastically different results with respect to overall cloud strategy?

Muneer   Asking a technical architect about accounting is like asking a pig to lay an egg. I can try, but chances are I'm not going to do a great job of it. Seriously, I'm not an accountant, but I have worked closely with FP&A and Carolyn on the models. We always use a basic model and it has worked for years. I won't even pretend to know that world.

Kayla   This brings up a great point. I get the distinct impression that, although a lot of you were nodding when Jorg explained the two different methods, the real impact wasn't clear to a lot of the people in this room. He's speaking a different language, isn't he?

(Various team members nod in agreement.)

Here's the situation. For most companies, basic cash flow modeling with some form of understanding as to whether the net present value of the investment is positive or negative can work pretty well. But cloud changes the game significantly, and the lack of a cohesive cloud strategy is more than likely the root cause for all the issues you guys are having with your budgets and forecasting.

Charles   How can you be so sure of that, Kayla?

Kayla   I have examples that will clarify where Jorg is coming from and hopefully help you all understand how important this topic is. Take a look at this slide Carolyn created for an upcoming CRM project. Carolyn, why don't you explain the model on the screen?

SaaS Solution for CRM (Cash Flow)

Initiative	2014	2015	2016	2017	2018	TCO
CRM	$3,300,000	$660,000	$660,000	$660,000	$660,000	$5,000,000
Integration	$2,000,000	$50,000	$50,000	$50,000	$50,000	$2,200,000
Resources	$1,000,000	$1,000,000	$100,000	$100,000	$100,000	$2,300,000
Infrastr	$1,000,000	100,000	100,000	100,000	100,000	$1,400,000
Total						$10,900,000

5-year lifecycle (should match lifecycle for company)
Recurring cost year over year
No depreciation benefit on subscription solutions
Resources required to integrate and sustain
Infrastructure for networking, storage, business continuity still needed

© 2014, iSpeak Cloud

Carolyn   Sure. This is a simple costing model. It takes the cost of the CRM subscription, the resource and connector costs for burst capacity to implement the solution, the ongoing resources that are needed for maintenance, infrastructure required for additional networking capacity, and disaster recovery/business continuity planning. The bottom of the slide explains the expected life of the CRM tool to be five years and briefly what the additional costs are.

Kayla   Thank you. That was a great explanation. I've asked Cody from Jorg's FP&A team to redo your numbers using a P&L model. Jorg can you explain the model on the screen?

SaaS Solution for CRM (P&L)

Initiative	2014	2015	2016	2017	2018	TCO
CRM (OpEx)	$1,000,000	$1,000,000	$1,000,000	$1,000,000	$1,000,000	$5,000,000
Integration (CapEx)	$1,600,000	$0	$0	$0	$0	$1,600,000
Integration (OpEx)	$400,000	$50,000	$50,000	$50,000	$50,000	$600,000
Resources (OpEx)	$200,000	$200,000	$100,000	$100,000	$100,000	$700,000
Resources (CapEx)	$800,000	$800,000	$0	$0	$0	$1,600,00
Infrastr (CapEx)	$800,000	$0	$0	$0	$0	$800,000
Infrastr (OpEx)		$150,000	$150,000	$150,00	$150,000	$600,000
Integration (D)	-$320,000	-$320,000	-$320,000	-$320,000	-$320,000	-$1,600,000
Resources (D)	-$320,000	-$320,000	-$320,000	-$320,000	-$320,000	-$1,600,000
Infrastr (D)	-$160,000	-$160,000	-$160,000	-$160,000	-$160,000	-$800,000
Total						$6,900,000

$ Jorg The obvious difference is that the cost is much lower with this model when looking at overall profit and loss.

Kayla Okay, but let's talk about *why* the numbers are so far apart. Think of it this way. Carolyn speaks English and Cobry speaks Spanish. We need an explanation in Spanglish to help both sides see why one model would paint such a drastically different financial picture.

$ Jorg I can give the high-level view on benefits of one over the other. That may help. The P&L model includes depreciation benefits from the solutions we own. I stress *own*. If you notice, our SaaS-based CRM solution is not depreciated. We receive depreciation benefits only from improvements, new solutions or integrations to our existing solutions. Since the solution is expected to have a five-year lifecycle, our fixed asset accounting team would have taken the cost of the depreciable assets, divided them over the five-year lifespan and deducted the costs as a write-off from revenue.

Carolyn So, the lower costs in my model come from a reduction in taxes?

Jorg	Exactly. We spread the costs over the life of the asset. This is a double-edge sword. As a company, we have to balance what's more important, a stronger cash position or longer-term savings and profits reported to the street.
Muneer	Not to be thick about this, but why do we care about this one? From what I can see, Carolyn's model was fine. It had higher stated costs, so in the end the cash-flow model is good because we should fare better in the end once the FP&A team works its magic on the numbers.
Kayla	Let me try another way to explain it. The model up on the screen is a mixed model with some on-premise components and some off-premise. So you're seeing the depreciation benefits. Jorg, what if all the infrastructure, integrations and other depreciable components in the model were outsourced to third parties? What would the impact be?
Jorg	That's easy. There would be no depreciation benefit. No tax savings. Everything would be OpEx and all the expenses would hit during the year they were incurred. We would not be able to stretch it out over the five years.
Muneer	Why not? We are still using the product for that five years.
Jorg	True, but we don't actually own anything. It's like renting a house. When you make improvements on third-party software and solutions, the third party owns the improvements.
Muneer	So even the resources would not be deductible?
Jorg	That's right. You can't deduct the interest your landlord paid on the mortgage. You essentially make all the payments but the landlord has all the liability and ownership. This is why our models are off. Every time someone in development or operations arbitrarily decides between on premise, where we own the solution, versus off premise, where the vendor owns it, there's a huge financial impact.

What's worse, although Carolyn did a good job in this example of the model, very few business people actually calculate the anticipated volumes in data that need to traverse the network. In other words, they completely overlook the need for increased infrastructure to support the increased traffic and higher ISP charges. That's a big reason we're constantly finding ourselves way over budget.

Muneer   Now I'm getting it. Now I understand why we've seen an exponential increase in network traffic despite the fact that the number of customers and business users have decreased over the last year in the trading line of business. It never made sense to me, but now it's becoming very clear.

Cobry   So, what I'm hearing is that these SaaS solutions we're deploying may not be saving as much as we think.

Jorg   Bingo. The same holds true for other solutions like infrastructure as a service. If you host something in Amazon or another third-party cloud, there can be a ton of benefits, but there will not be depreciation benefits.

Marissa   So how do we decide which route to take?

Kayla   Remember the chart I gave you earlier about creating our own cloud positioning system? This would incorporate the cost aspect. There are times when third-party hosted solutions make perfect sense. The example Cobry and Jorg are discussing is different. If the business is working around IT to the tune of 300 applications — maybe more — then people are not breaking out OpEx and CapEx expenses and treating them appropriately. By default the company is not receiving the depreciation benefit that it could based on the development work done to integrate SaaS solutions to on-premise systems. Nor is it accounting for the additional expenses based on virtual environments hosted in a cloud and charged to someone's corporate credit card. This leads to bigger issues that translate into a lack of visibility and transparency on the part of executive leadership. What are some other issues you have seen or could see based on this discussion? Andrew?

Andrew   From an audit perspective, we could have some issues with regulatory compliance. All of these things apparently impact the general ledger. With laws like Sarbanes Oxley, we have to be careful about anything that can have a material impact on the general ledger. Things like depreciation. And anything above $100,000 is considered material for our company.

> **Regulatory compliance**:
>
> Improper reporting of depreciation can have a material impact on general ledger and create compliance issues.

So, here's an example. Let's say you have 10 people officially assigned to operations. So accounting is treating their salaries as operating expense. But if they're actually spending most of their time on developing new applications or "assets," then a larger portion of their time should be classified as CapEx. Add up all those salaries, and that's a material impact.

Kayla   That's an area I hadn't even thought of. But you are spot on. And if you shift a system from on premise to cloud and you don't shift the associated costs from CapEx to OpEx, you would impact the integrity of the GL. Regardless of the models you use, if the information is incorrect or, in the case of shadow IT, not being tracked accurately, you will unknowingly violate laws like Sarbanes Oxley.

Cobry   I never thought of it that way. I think we were all just trying to get the job done and not worried about tracking some of these other areas. We have some really talented employees. They are really creative. I never thought about how what they were doing would affect the tracking of custom-developed pieces or the components we're hosting on third-party providers.

Kayla   Cobry, don't feel bad. Nearly every company I've worked with comes to this same realization. People get frustrated because they want to get work done. And when you're dealing with bright digital natives who are used to more advanced technologies from their consumer devices, they start looking for ways to get more. It's never malicious. As the representative for the business, though, you now have to consider the impact of shadow IT and help enforce the changes that come out of this workshop. As of today, you can no longer claim you don't know that what your team is doing is negatively affecting the company.

Cobry   This has definitely been an eye opener. I honestly was trying to cut through the red tape to help my people resolve customer issues. How do we enable people without breaking the accounting rules?

Elizabeth   Easy. Start following the processes we have put in place and work closely with the executive program management office to track expenditures. If you work with us instead of around us, we can track costs appropriately and accurately.

Charles   I, for one, am glad that one of my most senior business leaders gets it. Cobry, I'm expecting you to be the change agent to help your peers understand. One mandate that I will impose out of this meeting is that all uses of technology resources beyond standard maintenance through the service desk has to be vetted through the program management office.

Kayla   Is it clear now why each of you was selected to attend this workshop?

Rahul   Most definitely. It's really clear that we all have to work together to put the high-level guidelines in place. Otherwise we're hurting ourselves and pulling down the profitability of Universal Kingdom. Basically, if what I understand from this conversation is correct, without the appropriate guard rails to create a cloud positioning system, we will hit major issues with compliance, accounting and budgets, and we'll stall our overall efforts.

Kayla   That's very insightful, Rahul. Now let's take that and expand upon it for a bit. Many companies hit sprawl and then stall because they are working in silos. Each group thinks it knows best what the company needs. And groups do know what's best for their respective areas. Unfortunately, they aren't looking at the bigger picture.

Cobry   Implementing a perfect strategy is not realistic in a fast-moving environment like this. It will paralyze the company.

Kayla   Let's not be overly dramatic at this point. It's true that most enterprises are brownfield, not greenfield. Change at this level is nearly, and I stress *nearly*, impossible to obtain quickly. The only way you can fast track the change is with full support from the top, with both business and technology working together. The whole premise of business service management was to bridge the gap between technology and the business to enable the business services to drive technology roadmaps. We have to start somewhere or the company will continue to face insurmountable challenges that lead to lost profits and violations of regulations.

Cobry   Can you give us an example of other companies that hit this?

Kayla   One large communications company I worked with had issues very similar to yours. The cloud team implemented general rules and guidelines that gave choices for the business and technologists. If they wanted to use a third-party provider they could. However, the approach had to be approved as part of a larger project or proven to be necessary to ensure that agility was maintained to meet certain criteria.

Elizabeth   Can you recap the key points from this area? As you stated, this is a tough one. Did anyone bring ibuprofen? All this self-actualization reminds me of psychology class. If I didn't know better, I'd swear someone is going to start espousing Maslow's hierarchy of needs.

We are not quite ready for the recap as we haven't gotten through all the material yet. Let's break for lunch and, when we return, we can continue to cover the other aspects of the cloud cost calibration.

Afternoon Session: Asset Implications

Objectives

Provide a basic understanding of the implications on assets, cost structures and other factors that affect the overall cloud strategy business case.

Session Background/Overview

By the end of the afternoon session, you will understand:

- How cloud computing has fundamentally changed the traditional business case and affects the overall asset management structure
- How to determine if the "juice is worth the squeeze" when creating business case for cloud strategy

The Action

(Team returns from lunch and Kayla pulls up the following slide.)

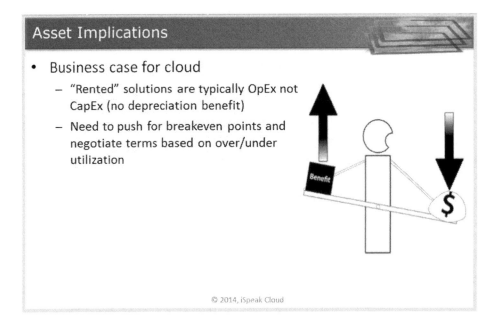

Kayla   Good afternoon. How are we doing? Any epiphanies over lunch? Let's start with a recap of the key concepts we covered this morning. Remember, the technology leaders are not expected to create the business case or accounting rules any more than the business is expected to write the code. They are, however, expected to understand key areas that need to be thought through.

Rahul   Well, that's a relief. Developers are great at math, so they could easily handle that role. But we don't want to distract them from getting the code developed.

Jorg   Yes, Rahul, without a doubt. I always knew you wanted to work for me.

Kayla   Well, since you two decided to start the discussion, can you both take a stab at the recap?

Rahul   Sure. Jorg, why don't you go first?

Jorg   In general, a P&L business case is better than a simple cash flow, although both are important. Each role has to contribute to the overall business case for it to be truly accurate and effective. If you put garbage into the equation, garbage is what you'll get out of it.

Rahul   Love that last line. We say the same about coding. Garbage in. Garbage out. Other key elements we took away from this morning is that CapEx is important because it means depreciation, which reduces our tax liability. We also learned that shadow IT not only hurts IT, but also the company as a whole. My favorite takeaway from this morning is that Cobry, our biggest shadow IT proponent, is now our evangelist in the fight against it.

Kayla   Not sure Cobry signed up for the last one, but he would be the ideal spokesperson. Now let's move on, shall we? One point that was not recapped was the whole notion that what you rent cannot be included in CapEx. This includes improvements on code and structure. Like a rental home, they don't belong to you. However, you can typically categorize integrations to legacy or on-premise solutions owned by Universal Kingdom to CapEx. There are a few more scenarios and planning components I'd like each of you to think about. First, let's talk about breakeven points. Muneer, can you tell us what breakeven is?

Muneer   The point in the contract when the license subscription justifies the expense?

Kayla   Close, but not quite. Ben, do you want to give it go?

Ben   I'm cheating a little and looking at your slide. The information there is limited, but I'd say the breakeven point would account not only for SaaS but could include IaaS. It would be the point when the investment in the people, process and technology has crossed over from being a cost to a benefit.

Kayla   Great explanation, Ben. I make another point on the slide regarding buying seats for a SaaS or IaaS solution. First, there's nothing worse than

> For SaaS and IaaS, monitor utilization and understand volumes to avoid under/overallocation.

purchasing thousands of licenses that end up not being used. So if you do go with a subscription model, you need a solid understanding of volumes needed. You want to avoid underallocation and overallocation. In other words, monitor utilization and understand your environment enough to time it appropriately.

Second, it's critical to have a clause in your subscription agreements that allows you to re-evaulate and either pivot

> Negotiate contracts with an escape clause to increase or decrease licenses.

licenses up or down until the system is completely deployed. I've worked with companies that didn't have these clauses. I'm sad to say, some of them spent millions on software that was not deployed but still in development due changes in the market, personnel, the company or, in some cases, vendors.

Charles	That is a critical point. What if we're already stuck with subscription contracts that don't have escape clauses?
Kayla	I'd talk to the vendor. A company your size can typically negotiate changes to the contract. If not, as soon as the subscription ends, add the clauses to the new contract or switch vendors.
	Let's talk about additional asset implications such as the duration of the business case. Can someone tell me why I chose five years for the example instead of the standard three or four?
Marissa	Because the depreciation lifecycle for the CRM product is on the books for five years?
Kayla	Depreciation is part of it, but also you should think about how long the company will typically use the solution. This is a critical factor in choosing your route to value — whether it's SaaS, IaaS or an on-premise solution for either licenses or cloud. One customer I worked with chose a SaaS solution because the business case was created using a three-year model for CRM. At first blush it appeared to be a better deal than purchasing an on-premise solution. However, when the business case was extended an additional two years, it was obvious that the on-premise solution was the way to go. Can anyone guess why?
Carolyn	The longer you leverage an application and/or underlying infrastructure, the more sense it makes to own it. I'll use the rental home analogy again. If you're going to be in an area for only a short time, the startup costs and maintenance are higher if you're buying than if you're renting. The converse is also true. The longer you keep the home — or, in this case, the software — the more advantageous it is to own it.
Kayla	That is a perfect segue for the law of diminishing returns. Andrew, can you add to Carolyn's analogy?

Asset Implications

Law of Diminishing Returns
- Gift that keeps on giving
  - Yearly costs versus one time
  - Resources required to integrate, own, manage hybrid

- Is the juice is worth the squeeze?
  - Larger enterprise show savings based on existing infrastructure and traditional license models
  - Costly to redo environment if you change cloud providers

© 2014, iSpeak Cloud

Andrew   It sounds like you will hit a point where renting — or, in the case of software, choosing the subscription model — no longer makes sense and it's smarter to buy.

Kayla   Exactly. Not long ago, the CIO of a major healthcare organization asked me why a particular implementation was so much higher than what he had seen at other organizations. The answer was simple: Public cloud is the gift that keeps on giving. Meaning, you lose the depreciation benefit and the costs don't go down.

In some cases, costs unexpectedly increase year over year because the business case failed to account for all the costs. One factor that often gets missed is migration time from an application or solution in the cloud to another infrastructure. In the case of the healthcare company, management had planned to use the application for only three years. But the business case didn't account for the 18 months it would take to migrate onto and off of the application — for a grand total of 36 months. In this case, the period covered by the business case should have been at least six years, and the company

Charles   Kayla, that next bullet about brownfield versus greenfield, I'm really interested in that. Can you elaborate on that?

Kayla   This is one of my favorites. It's one of the biggest mistakes made in building a business case. People assume that because you are moving to either a SaaS or IaaS model, that the resources currently working on those solutions can be let go. I've seen some companies take a SWAG, or silly wild-ass guess, as to how many people are working on these systems. At one company, the manager doing the business case estimated he could let go 15 percent of the IT staff by implementing a SaaS solution on Amazon. There were two big mistakes here. Only nine percent of the staff was actually working on the software or infrastructure for the system. And, to add insult to injury, the team didn't account for the fact that IT would need resources to integrate the new solution to backend legacy systems and to accommodate business continuity or disaster recovery. Any guesses as to what happened in this scenario?

 Ben   They got the funding and signed the contract?

Kayla   Yep. Senior leaders quickly discovered that the business case was not nearly as good as everyone thought. The executives who were trying to make their numbers cut the employees according to the plan. Needless to say, the implementation did not go well. The first time there was an outage, the CIO lost his job because there was no disaster recovery plan in place to bring the systems back. By the time the consultants and vendors came in to salvage what they could, the project had cost the company three times the original estimate and delivered only 50 percent of the value originally called out.

But I'm also aware of a global logistics company that had siloed so much of their software decision making to local teams and business groups that only a SaaS offering could have turned them around within the short window they had — especially considering the incredibly small team of centralized IT resources. Their SaaS development platform rolled out quickly, united global teams, helped them design in corporate standard recovery plans for every application and saved them more than $80 million a year in unneeded and uncoordinated infrastructure and cloud costs. So SaaS can be a great asset in the right circumstances.

What is the lesson to be learned from these examples?

Cobry Don't allow decision making in silos, don't cut too deeply when making transitions and be sure to include plans for implementation resources.

Marissa Never roll anything into production without a solid disaster recovery and business continuity plan. Per your slide earlier, all data centers, including data centers run by cloud providers, will have an outage of some sort eventually. So you better plan for contingencies.

Kayla Okay, let's move on.

Rahul All right, Kayla, now you have to tell us what you mean by "is the juice worth the squeeze?" Who talks like that?

Kayla It's a throw back from my youth. My grandfather would speak that way — in very frank, matter-of-fact terms. A lot of times in life we are squeezed, either for resources or time. Just like squeezing lemons or oranges. Sometimes the juice, the fruit of your labor, is just not worth the time it takes to squeeze it.

I worked with one healthcare company that initially decided to build everything on a third-party cloud. This was a smaller company, and management felt it would remove the headache of the infrastructure. So IT worked with a small cloud service broker to build a vertical application. At first the business case made sense given the company's size and given the need to start getting value right away. However, as the company grew, so did consumption of the virtual machine environment.

Before long, senior leaders realized they had far surpassed the law of diminishing returns. For a company of that size and VM consumption, migrating to an on-premise private cloud would cost nearly 40 percent less. Bottom line: The juice received from the relationship with the provider was far less than what the company could get from an internal or on-premise cloud. Volume often changes the equation.

Rahul   So, are you saying that we should re-evaluate the environment to see if the business case for that solution still makes sense?

Kayla   Exactly. The company should understand what the key performance indicators are for a given service and monitor them for changes to ensure the value is still there. In some cases, I've seen customers recreate cloud provider environments because of the savings. Companies are like children. As they grow their needs change. The environment has to change accordingly. Just as a child moves from elementary school to junior high to high school, the environment you have for a particular service or system will most likely have to change over time. It's only a problem if you don't take that potential for change into account.

> Companies grow and change, so monitor KPIs regularly and determine if adapting or changing the environment makes sense.

Charles   How often should we reevaluate the plan?

Kayla   I recommend reviewing the plan at least quarterly. Ideally, each project will roll up into an overall program and each program into a prioritized initiative. The KPIs should have a similar roll-up using some form of dashboard. This kind of visibility lets leadership see how the solution is progressing and whether or not it's meeting objectives. Please note, these plans are often much more complex than the examples I've shown you today. Each service portfolio rolls across the horizontal cloud solution. It's important to evaluate at the service level and then aggregate to the value of the cloud.

Charles How should we incent teams to work toward this cohesive plan? Technology leaders have been talking about the silos for decades, but it appears that things haven't really changed as much as we'd like to believe.

Kayla Several companies I've worked with have shifted incentive bonuses to a P&L basis across the business and technology. They are achieving good results with this approach. They put the business and program management offices in charge of identifying efficiencies and building the business elements of the business case. The technology team, then, is responsible for design, delivery and quality. The primary leads for business, program, development, operations and product all are accountable for a given program. They're tasked with making the deadlines and numbers they agreed to when they built the business case. This forces collaboration and working across silos.

Rahul That sounds like a great approach for external projects or initiatives, but what about internal ones such as DevOps? How do they stack up against the projects that involve business units?

Kayla All internal projects such as DevOps should support initiatives that lead ultimately to business service success. For example, a private cloud initiative or hybrid cloud initiative should be justified as a horizontal service that supports CRM, email or other services you provide to the business. Each layer in the stack is interdependent and they all feed on each another — particularly horizontal solutions like cloud computing. In fact, there are a lot of factors that should feed into decision making in this process, from understanding the costs and benefits of how the services will use your cloud environment to regulatory, efficiency and impact to business velocity.

In the quest for cloud, I've seen some huge blunders when things were done the wrong way and, conversely, some major successes when things were done correctly. For example, a large telecommunications provider showed significant savings by migrating systems from third-party cloud providers and internal virtual environments to a private cloud. It took building a custom layer for migrating proprietary virtual environments, but the savings were worth the effort. The cost per month per VM dropped from $80 a month to $50.

Rahul   How do you approach building the case for internal projects like that one?

Kayla   Well, there are two ways you can tackle it. Ideally, you start by taking business cases built for services and then determining, based on routes to cloud value, what is most effective and efficient for the business. Unfortunately, in situations where the BSM business cases don't exist or where there is quite a bit of shadow IT, it's a bit more of a challenge. But the bottom line is, for your particular situation, you would start by analyzing the true total cost of ownership across the current services the company offers.

Rahul   For a large company like ours, with multiple subsidiaries, it feels more than a little overwhelming. How would you suggest we approach developing our cloud solution?

Kayla   Rahul, you're right. It can be daunting for a company the size of Universal Kingdom, and one with as many shadow IT issues as you have to deal with. The best approach is to start small and work your way out to a larger initiative.

One approach I've seen that is very effective is to target a large initiative such as the CRM one that was raised earlier. Look at projected costs, plan for implementation of infrastructure and apply modeling on potential savings with various cloud offerings — private, public and hybrid. Expand on that model with one or two smaller projects to determine if the "juice is worth the squeeze." This way you can project or at least come up with a process or methodology to calibrate your cloud vision.

Starting with new projects helps because the decision to make the investment in the service is already there for the company. So you have an opportunity to refine the business case by showing additional value or savings through enhancing your implementation planning. We'll be mapping more of this out tomorrow during our final session on cloud calibration. After our break there are four more concepts to cover. They'll assist us in getting through our final session tomorrow.

Afternoon Session (continued): Cloud Cost Challenges

Objectives

Provide a basic overview of the hidden costs, challenges and end-of-life considerations needed to determine the tradeoffs and the approach for a cloud strategy.

Session Background/Overview

By the end of this session, you will understand the following:

- Hidden costs associated with the various types of clouds
- Implications of costs creating challenges for business case, business and IT
- How to calculate, incorporate, and leverage end-of-life benefits as a part of a comprehensive cloud strategy

The Action

(Committee members take a seat as Kayla displays a slide on cost challenges.)

Cloud Cost Challenges

Hidden Costs

- Monitoring across clouds
  - Up doesn't mean it is working
- Infrastructure
  - Shifting costs/workload from systems to network
  - Latency impact to users/employees
- Support of hybrid models
  - Business continuity for 3rd parties
  - Level 3 triage requirements
  - Time to value against DevOps

© 2014, iSpeak Cloud

 Kayla   Good afternoon. Hopefully all of you have been able to tend to those pressing emails and voicemails and put out the fires and you're now ready to focus on this afternoon's session. So, our four topics related to cloud cost challenges are:

- Hidden costs

- Forecasting, or what I like to call "vision versus reality"

- End-of-life benefits and drawbacks, and

- Cloud tipping points

Let's start with the hidden costs that are often overlooked until you are in the middle of an implementation. Rahul, can you give us a few examples of hidden costs you've encountered?

Rahul   I'd say the biggest one is latency. We had to create a caching store on premise for one solution because the amount of time it was taking to launch the initial application for our stockbroker application was way too long. Over five minutes.

Kayla   Why did that happen? Ben?

Ben   The biggest gap we discovered was the dang school kids impacting response times.

Kayla   So, you have school kids using stockbroker applications? Not impossible for a Finance class. I know schools are progressive. But how are school kids actually impacting *your* network?

Ben   It's not as crazy as it sounds. You see, kids get out of school at about noon our time, which is 3:00 pm on the East coast. They immediately jump on the Internet to play their multimedia games, connect on social sites and watch videos. There was definitely a spike in latency of page rendering for our SaaS-based solution after 12 o'clock. We're convinced it was a result of the kid's gaming activity that was eating up bandwidth on the Web.

Kayla   Great point, Ben. What about the end-user machines?

Ben   We also learned the hard way that running a web-based application doesn't mean you can avoid upgrading end-user machines. Our SaaS provider made a big deal of the fact that we could extend the life of our existing machines. Unfortunately, that turned out not to be the case. Some of the calls from the web-based application and rendering process were so intense that we had to upgrade processing power. We also needed to upgrade the operating system to support later versions of the PDF and programming languages. So we didn't save nearly as much as we expected. In fact, it cost us more than it should have because we discovered the problems once we got into production. The pilot machines had already been replaced so they were fine. It was the machines on the floor that got us into trouble.

Kayla   Ben, that's a great example of how a cloud-based SaaS solution could impact the client solution and call center at the same time. As you look around the table, think about how your current projects could inadvertently impact each other. And the dependency you all have on each other's success.

Rahul, do you have another example?

Rahul Aggregation of tools and data is a hidden cost around hybrid monitoring tools. We had to customize our current web and internal application monitoring tools to work together to accommodate a project that used both on-premise legacy solutions and SaaS solutions. To calculate whether or not we were delivering on the SLAs and have visibility into whether or not the service was actually functioning as committed, we had to extend our current tools quite a bit.

Kayla Why is that? Couldn't the tools you already had ping the web applications?

Rahul Yes, but we found out that doesn't necessarily tell you that the service is working. For example, we had the ping capability set up for our pilot CRM solution. The site was responding to the ping, telling us it was up. But none of the functions on the page were working properly. We had to work with the vendor to get APIs that gave us more intelligent messaging to provide visibility into whether or not the site was fulfilling service obligations.

Kayla Thank you, Rahul. You actually tied together two of the hidden cost challenges on my slide: the monitoring tools and triaging third-party support tools. Who wants to talk about the next one — time to value against DevOps? Rahul?

Rahul I am not sure that relates. Our DevOps initiatives don't hinder these services. DevOps helps them.

Marissa Hmmm. Not sure the business would agree with that statement. The call center is swarming with calls any time our organizational development team isn't involved in managing the implementation and training for major changes being introduced.

Cobry   I agree with Marissa. DevOps definitely impacts the business and operations. We have no issues with underlying infrastructure changes, but we do have issues when applications or processes are changed without notice. Or when major releases or features hit production without the business being involved. It's very disruptive to our employees.

Kayla   I see we have brought up a very touchy subject. I'm not surprised you're experiencing these issues because a lot of people confuse some of the concepts of DevOps in their implementation. DevOps is about the development team and operations working closely together and development taking more of an instrumental role in supporting the products they roll to production. There are great benefits. Faster response, shorter implementation cycles and higher efficiency are just a few. But there are drawbacks when DevOps isn't implemented correctly.

The hidden costs come in here from time lost when users try to figure out where a link or feature went, or when one infrastructure element breaks another in production because testing wasn't rigorous enough.

What I'm saying is DevOps is a great initiative but only if it's done right. You can't bypass best practices while you're on the road to continuous delivery. Otherwise hidden costs creep in because you have a higher number of errors throughout the system. I know I keep harping on this, you'll spend about 1/100th the amount to address an error in development than you'll spend if you have to address it in production. The more users are affected, the higher your hidden costs.

Suriya   I'd like to add something. It isn't just the errors that impact users and costs. We had an instance where development changed the colors of an icon for an application. It was an intentional change related to a new branding initiative. But when the users saw it, they were so worried it was a virus, they wouldn't run the application. Instead they flooded the help desk with calls. If we had known about the change ahead of time, we could have been proactive. We could have notified the users and, for people who didn't see the notification, our call center agents would have been prepared to explain that the new icon was fine.

Kayla   Very good point. Okay, let's go on to the issue of competing initiatives impacting your implementation. Anyone have an example?

$ Jorg   I do. A database upgrade across the board delayed our ERP system upgrade by two months. The same resources that were working on the database upgrade needed to work on the ERP system. Because the databases needed to be updated first, we had to wait. When the business case was presented to the executive staff and timelines were discussed, there was no mention of the need for an upgrade.

Kayla   That is a good example on many fronts. First of all, there was no tracking of the impact of interdependent work streams with respect to time to value and cost. Second, there was no consideration given to the fact that you have multiple projects competing for resources. I've seen cases where employees are either stretched too thin or they're bored because they are waiting for another part of the project to be completed. It sounds like your ERP resources were in a holding pattern while the database engineers didn't get much of a break between projects.

This can affect costs in a bigger way because fatigue causes more errors and increased risk of attrition.

This is a good transition to the next topic, forecasting. Jorg, based on your example, why is accurate forecasting important?

$ Jorg Well it's pretty clear that competing priorities can lead to some people being overworked and some being underworked. You're probably not getting optimum value from your resources and your costs are not accurate.

Kayla Exactly. One critical part of forecasting is what I call integration, tuning and timing or ITT. Essentially, these competing service business cases need to be tightly managed and calibrated to forecast and reduce potential hot and cold spots that might impact resources and ultimately the business case.

Integration is creating a consolidated view across high-priority programs or initiatives. *Tuning* is adjusting those plans across competing programs based on time to value and cost benefit to the company. High-benefit, least-cost programs get higher priority.

Another part of tuning is identifying potential resource contention to minimize impact well in advance. Not just a day or a week before but at least four sprints out. That way you have enough cushion to allow the team two sprints of planning based on high-level directives.

Finally, let's talk about *timing*, which is understanding not only how much time it will take — your best estimate — but also adjusting based on time to value or the impact the solution has on the overarching cloud plan. Who wants to take a stab at the next bullet — the true cost of third-party tools?

Andrew I will. We see this from time to time. From our perspective, it's the administrative overhead that often isn't accounted for in resourcing. This is where shadow IT comes in. Meaning, often there is an administrative burden tied to applications — even SaaS — that we're not accounting for. Granting permissions. Counting licenses. Ensuring we are licensed to use a product a certain way.

(Kayla pulls up a slide.)

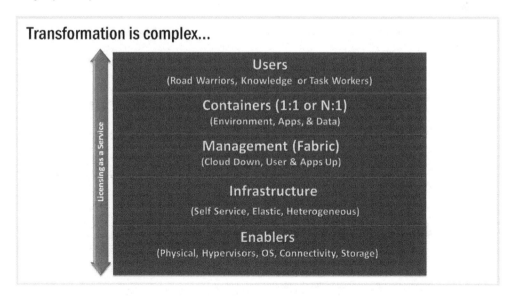

Kayla Great point. I thought I would bring out this graphic from a good book I read, *Client4Cloud*. It shows how complex the overall transformation is. To your point, Andrew, licensing affects every layer of the stack. But you typically have only limited resources and knowledge for tracking those licenses. My experience with enterprise customers shows that the problem becomes more unsettling with the cloud. Enterprises are already struggling to accurately track and correlate real software usage against the applications they are licensed for.

Often procurement is not the one deploying the licenses and so it's not always clear what the enterprise owns. Some vendors restrict applications or have special license agreements to leverage them on a third-party cloud.

So we have the perfect storm brewing among vendors, providers and their customers. Licensing as a service makes it even more interesting for enterprises to track how it stacks up against security and regulatory compliance due to the same restrictions. As you can see, you have to track multiple layers in the overall compute stack, and there's no easy way to do this in third-party clouds. That's why I believe open source is so attractive to companies.

Ⓘ Charles   Great point, Kayla. You know, we were hit with an unexpected $6 million in additional license fees last year when our vendor did a true up of licensed versus used applications on our internal systems. As a standard practice we try to sign up for enterprise license agreements to avoid the confusion you just described.

Kayla   Respectfully, Charles, I would say your solution doesn't fully solve the problem. Many ELAs don't transfer to third-party clouds. You would have had to negotiate using the software as part of the overall license agreement. I've seen companies hit with twice that number because the licenses they deployed in third-party clouds weren't covered. And the cloud provider worked with the vendor to provide reports on overage.

End-of-life Benefits

- Unless something comes out when you put something in, you're increasing expenses
- Writing off assets has hidden risks as well as rewards

© 2014, iSpeak Cloud

Rahul   Kayla, I'm interested in the end-of-life benefits. My team is really maxed out trying to support legacy applications. We haven't taken anything out. And we have to keep adding more applications to the stack. How should we handle this?

Kayla   At the business case level. Whenever you build a business case for a new service, be sure to calculate savings from retiring less efficient applications, servers, networking and other components. If you don't plan for end of life as part of the larger initiative, you may find the company moves on to the next big initiative before you've replaced enough to justify decommissioning the obsolete solution. A big part of the business requirements document is timing of not only when new systems roll into production but also when you pull the plug on old ones.

Jorg   How does that affect assets?

Kayla   One of the hidden risks with decommissioning is understanding what will be unplugged and when. If a particular application is being phased out in six months, it doesn't make sense to migrate it to cloud. You'd be surprised how many companies make this mistake. IT buys extra servers at $100,000 a pop to accommodate the application in the cloud infrastructure. And the staff spends all that time doing the migration. Once the application is decommissioned, people suddenly realize they're stuck with servers they really don't need.

We have one final topic before we call it a day. Marissa, do you want to try this one?

Cloud Cost Challenges

Tipping Point

- Each route to cloud value has a different tipping point
- There is no "one cloud fits all"
- Agility with a plan in mind

© 2014, iSpeak Cloud

 Marissa   This looks more like a summary from what we learned today. Essentially, each route to cloud value has a tipping point where one method or another no longer makes good business sense. Regardless of how agile we are, we still need to follow a large-scale plan that integrates, tunes and times solutions across the cloud. This is how we can figure out if the juice is worth the squeeze.

Kayla   Perfect! By the glossy eyes and blank stares, I'd say it's time to call it a day. Thank you all for your time. Remember, tomorrow is a critical session. We'll pull all these concepts together and complete our cloud positioning system.

Food for Thought

Action	Considerations
Create master planning solution	Do you currently have tools that track resources, projects, requirements and timelines? Can you create an automated update system through a portal or other customizable interface to those tools?
Input prioritized requirements into planning solution	Rank your business requirements based on value to the company (intrinsic and monetary) from the BRDs. Input or pull resources and velocity to meet service levels.
Calibrate timelines, resources and results	As a team, work out the priorities. Does everyone agree once they have viewed the integrations, tuning and timing required to make specific timelines? Are some projects affected due to interdependencies? What tradeoffs will need to be made to succeed?
Understand asset implications	What is the domino effect of cloud on your assets? Are there any resources or solutions you could capitalize that have changed since you switched to either a cloud infrastructure or hosted solution? Is the juice still worth the squeeze or have you (will you) hit the law of diminishing returns? Is there anything you want to do differently with this new data?

Understand and calculate cost challenges	Have you converted your ROI calculations to include depreciation and losses due to conversion from a capital expense to an operational expense? Do you have a clear understanding of integration, tuning and timing to know how this will affect your resources, costs and ability to forecast? Have you applied the iterative agile forecasting model to your requirements and resources to determine your timeline (25% new features, 25% hardening, 20% holidays/vacation/sick time pad, 30% new feature enhancements)? How has it affected your forecasts and plans?

Cloud Quest Workshop Day 3

Morning Session: Cloud Calibration

Objectives

Tie together all critical elements of the BRD, master planning template, approach and strategy from previous two days to create master cloud framework across siloed organizations.

Session Background/Overview

By the end of this session, you will be able to:

- Establish new policies and precedence defining who can do what, when, where and why, establishing service levels and ensuring transparency and tracking
- Determine what's possible or realistic to achieve based on current reality
- Finalize a roadmap that takes advantage of low-hanging fruit and encompasses integration, tuning and timing

The Action

(Kayla kicks off the morning session with the team as they settle in with their continental breakfast.)

Cloud Calibration (Vision to Reality)

Establishing New Policies and Precedence

- Who can do what, where, why, how
- Service levels and agreements across layers
- Transparency and tracking (chargeback, showback, SLAs)

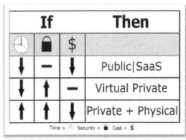

If			Then
⏲	🔒	$	
↓	—	↓	Public|SaaS
↓	↑	—	Virtual Private
↑	↑	↓	Private + Physical

Time = ⏲ Security = 🔒 Cost = $

©iSpeakCloud, 2013

© 2014, iSpeak Cloud

Kayla Good morning, everyone. I hope you're all well rested after yesterday's exercises and homework. The good news is you have made it this far and covered quite a bit of ground on your journey. The downside is you still have one more day until you can test out your "mad cloud" skills. Today, we'll tie all the concepts together from the last few days and create a plan to move forward on Universal Kingdom's cloud strategy.

Charles Team, I realized how busy everyone is, but please remember that this last session is crucial. Pay close attention because, at the end of today, all of you will have calls to action and responsibility for implementing your part of the overall strategy for the journey to the cloud.

Kayla Thank you, Charles. Now, based on the slide that's up on the screen, can someone tell us what today's objectives are?

Rahul Is it pulling together our baseline plan for a cohesive cloud strategy?

Kayla   Close but not quite. It's creating the starting point and initiating dialog. However, today is all about calibration. We need to calibrate resources, requirements and constraints to determine the best routes to value moving forward. There are three overarching steps to cloud calibration. Carolyn, can you tell us what they are?

Carolyn   Kayla, you're making this way too easy on us. But after the mind-numbing number crunching yesterday, it's much appreciated. The three steps on the slide are:

- Establishing new policies and precedence

- Discovering the art of possible

- And creating the roadmap for your cloud journey

Kayla   Very well said. If I didn't know better I would swear you were a mind reader. (I mean slide, not mind.) These concepts should be very familiar because we've been working on all three of them over the past two days. Now let's take a journey into workshops past? What did we talk about on the first day that we can leverage to create policy and precedence?

Rahul   We did a lot more than talk. We built a decision tree with policies defining who can do what, where, when and how. We leveraged these policies along with service level agreements and determined that we need to have, at a minimum, a method for allocating who is utilizing what resources so can charge back or show back the costs for each project and program.

Kayla   Excellent. How about you, Ben? Can you tell us what the decision tree looks like for your group and how you'll use it to calibrate cloud strategy?

Ben   Sure. Here's the decision tree for data center operations. The example of when to allow resources to leverage third-party providers is a great one.

Cloud Decision Tree Example

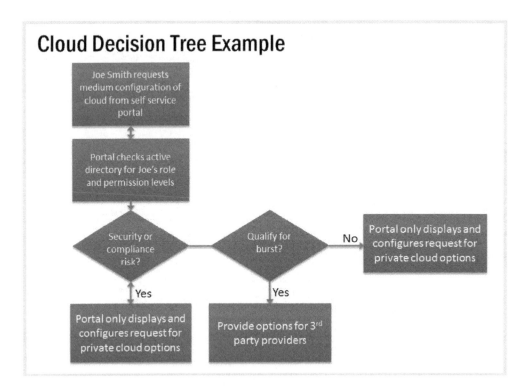

Kayla   Ben, before you dive into the example, can you elaborate on the constraints and challenges you tried to address with these new policies?

Ben   I guess you're not going to be as easy on me as you were on Carolyn. Okay. I'm recalling several challenges mentioned at the kickoff of this workshop. Taming the hybrid hydra is one of them. Balancing conflicting trends around regulatory compliance, agile computing, cloud and DevOps is another. The final challenge is implementing the changes cloud will require, working within the confines of our current fragile IT systems. A complete overhaul all at once isn't possible.

Kayla   Charles, when you and I discussed setting up this workshop, you emphasized that Universal Kingdom has a very diverse set of requirements around products, services and regulatory compliance. You told me that you were brought in as CIO to address four primary corporate objectives. These are the objectives that this group needs to keep in mind as they work on identifying a course of action for cloud computing. Can you take a few minutes to familiarize everyone with those objectives?

Cloud Strategy Objectives

- Increase time to value of key business initiatives
- Bring transparency around P&L of current technology portfolio investments
- Address compliance concerns
- Cut IT spend by 30%

© 2014, iSpeak Cloud

Charles   Sure. As you see in the slide, there are four of them. They are simple to understand, but we'll have to work together to achieve them. Our objectives are:

- Increase time to value of key business initiatives impacting market competitiveness

- Bring transparency around profit and loss of current technology portfolio investments

- Address compliance concerns raised by audit

- Cut IT spend by 30 percent

Kayla   Now, Ben, with those challenges and objectives in mind, tell us how your example will help this team stay on track.

Cloud Calibration (Vision to Reality)

Establishing New Policies and Precedence

- Who can do what, where, why, how
- Service levels and agreements across layers
- Transparency and tracking (chargeback, showback, SLAs)

If			Then
🕐	🔒	$	
↓	—	↓	Public|SaaS
↓	↑	—	Virtual Private
↑	↑	↓	Private + Physical

Time = 🕐   Security = 🔒   Cost = $

©iSpeakCloud, 2013

Ben   The graphic that Kayla has on the slide is the one that Carolyn, Muneer and I put together in our process mapping session on the first day. By creating a flowchart that we can automate via our existing runbook automation and customer relationship management tools, we can easily address the primary objectives while also overcoming key challenges.

The policies help us set up guard rails with checks and balances across business and technology. For example, the decision tree specifies that third-party cloud usage must be obtained from one of three approved providers. What's more, requests for these services have to be submitted and approved through the standard self-service portal we're already using for physically installed applications. Users have to select the cloud provider based on security and regulatory levels to minimize compliance risks. Employees working on regulated applications and data are directed to the provider with a virtual private cloud and direct-connection access instead of a public provider that doesn't have those security mechanisms.

Charles Sounds like a solid plan, Ben. When will it be instituted? Remember, vision without execution is hallucination.

Suriya The client operations team is working closely with Ben's team to implement the workflows and test them out operationally with our existing tools.

Charles Wait, you can use existing tools in the cloud? I thought that wasn't possible.

Suriya You can use them to a point, but usually there's quite a bit of integration and uplifting as part of the process. The key is to use open standard coding and processes. Open standards make it easier to transition forward.

Kayla Okay, let's keep moving. What's the next step in the cloud calibration process?

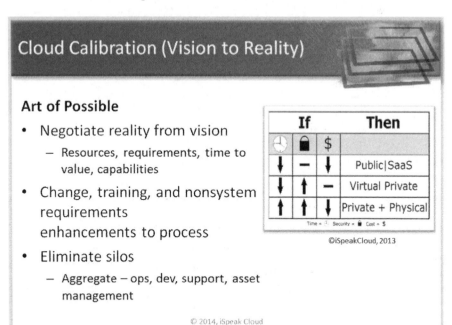

Carolyn Negotiate vision from reality. In other words, realistically review time to value and costs versus rewards, and then make sure you have a clear idea of what's actually needed along with the value the service provides. A critical component to this piece is the BRD, which should aggregate requirements that aren't feature related across the business, development and operations. This approach will enable a cohesive strategy across functional roles while eliminating silos.

Kayla   Excellent, Carolyn. Now let's talk about our journey to the cloud. Who wants to take a crack at reviewing what we have covered on that topic?

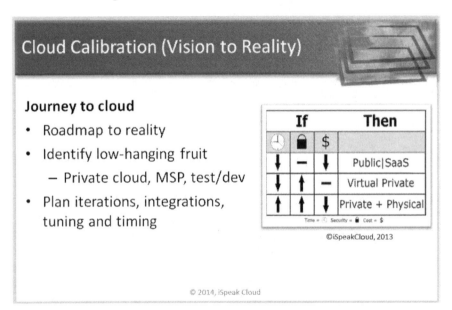

Elizabeth   Kayla, I have this one. As your slide says, the journey to the cloud requires a crawl-walk-run approach. We start with a small pilot project. We leverage the pilot to determine processes, interdependencies, integration, tuning and timing across multiple layers in the stack. This would include legacy, new cloud infrastructure, third-party clouds, mobile devices and remote workforce elements. The idea is to start small and pick the low-hanging fruit, and then use what we learn to guide us along the best pathway for the journey forward.

Kayla   Great explanation. Let's see who was paying attention and can provide an example of why managing the swim lanes is critical. Rahul?

Rahul   Well, I'd say an iterative agile approach enables you to understand enough about the requirements that you can plan your resources across multiple groups and roles. This is critical for shared resources such as our database and integration engineers who may be required to create solutions that tie various tools together. If we aren't careful in our implementation of agile, we'll end up with hot spots and cold spots in terms of people. The example you provided was the company where employees were leaving because they were either overworked or bored because they didn't have enough to do.

Kayla   Great review of the material. And now the fun begins. I think you'll agree that I've saved the best for last. For the remainder of the workshop, we'll split out into groups and create a cloud framework for Universal Kingdom. The idea is that by the end of today you'll have a blueprint addressing key challenges and achieving core corporate objectives.

The slide up on the screen shows the makeup of the three groups. Any questions?

Cloud Framework Teams

Business – Led by Product Management

- Governance – Legal; Audit & Compliance; Business Leads – Call Center, Services

Development – Led by Program Management with Product

- Engineering – Leads, Architects, QA; Financial Planning & Analysis; Security; Change Management

Operations – Led by Program Management with Product

- Infrastructure; Client; Change Mgmt & Service Desk

© 2014, iSpeak Cloud

Heidi	How do we ensure that each group has what it needs for a comprehensive plan?
Kayla	Two of you will act as liaisons across the groups to tie together the overarching plan. We want to mirror reality as much as possible. It isn't realistic to expect that this group will have the bandwidth on a regular basis to plan, execute and measure effectiveness of your strategy. It is realistic to create a monthly oversight committee led by two liaisons who tie the pieces of the puzzle together and make sure everyone stays on the same page. Make sense?
Heidi	Kind of.
Kayla	Good. Now let's discuss the subgroups: business, development and operations. The two liaisons are Carolyn and Elizabeth. Can anyone tell me why we picked this structure?
Ben	Because that's the way we are set up organizationally?

Kayla	Precisely. We don't want to change things so drastically that the groups feel uncomfortable or threatened. It's like when you lose weight. If you don't make true cultural changes, before long you revert to your old behaviors. Although this workshop has been great to get everyone on the same page, all of you still have to think in terms of your primary responsibilities. Given that product management is still a new function and project managers are being revamped, now is the perfect time to implement processes and determine how those processes can best be leveraged across teams.
Carolyn	Kayla, I see my team is listed quite a bit up there. We are more than happy to step up but that will be quite a bit of effort. What are the expectations here?
Kayla	Elizabeth's program management team will help with day-to-day execution and coordination with the exception of the business work that needs to be done. Your team is expected to create and update the master plan and provide direction based on information across the groups. Think of the business as your end customer and the other teams as your inbound teams to update requirements and create plans and business cases.
Carolyn	Got it! I just wasn't quite sure if we would be crossing any boundaries with other groups.
Kayla	Any other questions?
Rahul	Why is FP&A in the development group?
Kayla	Because the financial guys are your best source for pulling together costs, benefits and areas of concern. The FP&A guys watch costs, so they will be your first line to let you know if you're on target or not for the budget you're requesting or the budget that has been allocated. Other questions?
Cobry	I think we're good for now.

Kayla   Good. Take a minute to move around so that you're sitting with members of your group. Then we'll talk about this next slide.

Cloud Framework

- Select Service (low-hanging fruit, minimum 5 integrations)
- Build P&L Case
- Identify areas of investment
- Execute Pilot Project
    - Create, formalize and execute new cloud policies
    - Create knowledgebase & metrics – KPIs, service levels
    - Measure effectiveness
    - Integration, tuning and timing
- Expand to other areas of savings (highest first)
- Repeat

© 2014, iSpeak Cloud

Kayla   Is everyone ready? Let's get to work.

Ben   Kayla, shouldn't we all have a say in what service is selected?

Kayla   Absolutely. Everyone should have an opinion. The ultimate selection will depend on the outcomes of the exercises today. For example, how can you pick a service until you know whether or not the business case justifies the expense? Or whether or not the technology and skills available can support it.

So, task number one is for the teams take 15 minutes to recommend a service or list of services they consider to be low-hanging fruit. Carolyn and Elizabeth, you'll be the facilitators in helping to create the list.

(15 minutes later, Carolyn hands out copies of the list created by each group.)

Services

Operations

- Remote workforce with hosted virtual desktops
- Private Cloud
- Update Configuration Management Database to include Cloud and Mobile
- Upgrade Configuration Management software
- Database version upgrade
- Virtualization uplift project for Legacy Applications

Development

- DevOps
- Rewrite call center application to reduce support calls
- Upgrade Integrated Development Environment
- Create an Agile Development Lifecycle
- Implement new source code tracking system to increase efficiency
- Implement new program management & costing system to track efficiency and velocity of development teams
- Obfuscation of data in test equipment to reduce security breaches

Business

- Upgrade Customer Relationship Management system to reduce time in queue for incoming calls
- Upgrade online trading tool to reduce calls to support desk
- Implement electronic check cashing and signatures
- Implement chat and other forms of communications to service customer better
- Upgrade cloud implementations to follow new NIST standards

Kayla   So let's take a look, and I'd like for Carolyn or Elizabeth to tell us what stands out the most about the list?

Elizabeth   The priorities and services don't match.

Kayla   Exactly. The services deemed critical by each group differ considerably.

So, the next task is for each team to rank the list in order of importance. For those business leads like Cobry and Carolyn, can you please fill in any numbers you have for a P&L opportunity? You have 30 minutes for this exercise.

(After deliberating the potential cost savings and other benefits, the teams reduce the list to three initiatives.)

Services

- Rewrite Call Center Application (same as enhance call center application)
- Remote Workforce
- Private Cloud — with hybrid hooks

Kayla   Good work, you guys. But how did you reach this conclusion?

Carolyn   We had some preliminary numbers from the business on the savings we'd achieve if we automated some of the tasks. We used those numbers to calculate the business benefit — the profit the company would gain from implementing a solution.

Jorg   I also had a couple of my employees pull what we have on projected CapEx and OpEx from the ones that are budgeted. Ben and his team were really helpful as well. We were able to provide some preliminary costs from a high level.

Kayla   Excellent. Now take a look at this slide and let's talk about costs.

Cloud Framework Plans

- Business – Benefits & Requirements
  - Benefits – how will you gather the savings? Define time to value? Contingency planning?
  - What are key performance indicators ? What does success look like for the business?
  - How will you collect costs for business? For example, leads time to implement, change management, documentation, training, etc.

- Development – Technology Costs, Architecture, Contingencies
  - Technology - skills/training required to implement
  - Contingency plans based on desired time to value
  - Resources – burst, full time, part time, and savings

- Operations – Service & Change Management Cost, Measurements
  - Costs to maintain solution/service for lifecycle of the product
  - Technology, skills and resource requirements to implement/maintain new solution
  - Service Level Agreements and measurements – early & often

© 2014, iSpeak Cloud

Kayla   It's great that you have some preliminary numbers, and for the purpose of today's exercise that information will help. But as you get into your next steps, you'll need a more comprehensive cost breakdown to determine profit and loss.

Obviously, at this point, you're not going to have the full breadth and depth of numbers you'll need for a comprehensive cost model. So for the next exercise I'm going to ask each group for a plan on how it will set up the framework to capture the costs and benefits based on what you've learned to create that business case.

Break into your groups and take 30 minutes to create a plan. Then give your plans to Carolyn and Elizabeth so they can create a coordination framework for an overarching view. And please nominate a team leader to present your plan when they call on you. Any questions?

Ben   Kayla, are you asking us to know all the costs today?

Kayla   No, just come up with a plan as to how you'll get them. Who you will assign and why? What will you collect to fill in the business case? Remember, one of the biggest reasons I'm here is to help this group create a strategy and plan of execution to make your cloud initiative successful. One critical element is having a plan and being able to adjust it. We need to see if this team can break down the silos to achieve results that have been set forth. If not, we have to do some more work in that area. So get to work, and if you need help, feel free to call on me.

(About 15 minutes into the session Carolyn signals for Kayla to come over to the business team.)

Kayla   How can I help you, Carolyn?

Carolyn   We're a little confused on how what we're working on maps back to the other groups. Can you explain the connection points? This will help us create the plan.

Kayla   Of course. The connection points are the key. This group will come up with a ranked list of business requirements from a high level that you will build the benefits and savings on. For example, if automated screen pops with chat is a new capability that will help the company more than any other requirement, it would be listed as the first requirement. But stay away from the specific details on the "how" — the specifics of how many screen pops and how they will work — and focus more on the "what," as we discussed in our BRD session.

Cobry   Kayla, I am sorry but I'm still a little confused. Can you give us an example from what we covered the last few days that would help us?

Kayla   Sure.

(Kayla brings over her laptop and pulls up a slide showing how the master planning spreadsheet, P&L business case and BRD fit together.)

Cloud Framework Mapping

Business – Benefits & Requirements

- Map business plan / master plan / costs & savings in business case
- Tie back to BRD and metrics
- Business sets priority and numbering to tie back

#	Business Requirement	Value/$	Scale/ Priority
1	High level business benefit to be delivered by a given service or portfolio of services	High	1
2	Business Benefit #2 to be delivered by a given service or portfolio. For example, Business will be able to view account history	High	1

SaaS Solution for CRM (P&L)

Initiative	2014	2015	2016
CRM (OpEx)	$1,000,000	$1,000,000	$1,000,000
Integration (CapEx)	$1,600,000	$0	$0
Integration (OpEx)	$400,000	$50,000	$50,000
Resources (OpEx)	$200,000	$200,000	$100,000
Resources (CapEx)	$800,000	$800,000	$0
Infras (CapEx)	$800,000	$0	$0

© 2014, iSpeak Cloud

Kayla   Take a look at the slide and you'll see that the whole concept is around linking and synching the data to connect the dots across the silos. The first step in making that connection is getting everyone to agree on the low-hanging fruit. The second is to link and sync the high-level business requirements — the 50,000-foot level — to high-level costs to determine if a pilot makes sense at all.

The numbers won't be precise but they will help you cull the list of initiatives into something that makes sense — something that's achievable and will provide value to the company. This slide shows the connection between the high-level requirements and the business case.

A	B	C	E	F	G	H
#	Business Requirement	Value/$	Scale/ Priority	Actual Release	Target Release	Portfolio
1	High level business benefit to be delivered by a given service or portfolio of services	High	1		V 1	Product Portfolio A (CRM)
2	Business Benefit #2 to be delivered by a given service or portfolio. For example, Business will be able to view account history	High	1		V 1	Product Portfolio A
3	Business Benefit #3. For example, Business will be able to transfer customers from one service representative to another.	Med	1		V 1	Product Portfolio A
4	Business will be able to Identify & prioritize work for staff (ie. Work=automated contact strategy)	High	1		V3 (V2+)	Product Portfolio A/B (CRM/UCP)

If you look at the master planning sheet, which I have up on the screen now, you can see that every requirement is tied back to a service portfolio and subproducts that make up that portfolio. The business case then takes the costs associated with those products and breaks them down into quarterly expenses. The business case should include everything from the technology to the resources to implement the technology. Other key value inputs include savings from the business benefits, either due to resources being reallocated or eliminated, reduced operational expenses and reduced maintenance.

Cobry   Ahh. This is starting to make more sense now. So you're saying we need to tie it all together with the numbering system of the requirements?

Kayla   Yes, you need someone to show that the same business requirements are accurately reflected through linking and synching across the three critical elements.

> Link and synchronize requirements across:
>
> - The master plan (requirements/timelines)
> - The business case (savings and benefits versus cost)
> - The BRD (nonfeature requirements)

The master plan, which ties the details of resources, requirements and timelines together, the business case, which ties the savings or benefits of implementing the requirements back to the costs on a per-initiative basis, and the

BRD, which ties all nonfeature requirements back to these two other documents.

$ Jorg   How do we connect what we are working on with the technology team?

Kayla   That's the job of the people on the product team. They will be the translators between technology and the business. They will collect the costs, solutions and details from the technology team and the high-level business case from you. From there, they can determine whether to move forward or not.

The key is to remember that, with data, garbage in equals garbage out. Your high-level requirements and the costs of the technology have to be based in reality.

Carolyn, can you start collecting the various plans from the other groups so we can consolidate everything? Jorg, Cobry, don't forget, you need a spokesperson to articulate the plan. That can be Carolyn or someone else from your group.

Kayla   Okay, teams, you have 10 minutes to complete the assignment. If you need more time you can work on it over lunch. We're bringing in lunch today in case the teams need more time. In 30 minutes we'll review the overarching plan and discuss next steps.

Afternoon Session: Cloud Framework

Objectives

Review cloud framework exercises as a group to finalize the workshop and enable the executive team to determine next steps,

Session Background and/or Overview

By the end of this session, you will:

- Understand the different perspectives needed to create cohesive cloud framework across the three primary areas — business, engineering and operations
- Have a baseline framework to start from as an executive team to discuss finalization and execution strategy at the next staff meeting
- Determine next steps as a team and action items to prepare for staff

The Action

(Kayla kicks off the session by pulling up a slide and coaxing team members back into the room.)

Cloud Framework

- Select Service (low-hanging fruit, minimum 5 integrations)
- Build P&L Case
- Identify areas of investment
- Execute Pilot Project
    - Create, formalize and execute new cloud policies
    - Create knowledgebase & metrics – KPIs, service levels
    - Measure effectiveness
    - Integration, tuning and timing
- Expand to other areas of savings (highest first)
- Repeat

© 2014, iSpeak Cloud

Kayla   Good news. We're making great progress and we're almost done. If all goes well, we'll be out of here by 4:30. Just a few minutes ago, Carolyn asked a great question that I want to pose to this group. What happens to an initiative when you discover during this process that the juice is not worth the squeeze?

Jorg   It gets cut.

Rahul   Jorg, are you sure that's always the case? Many times we have to do a project for regulatory or other reasons. The savings aren't there, but we have to do the project anyway. For example, encryption of data at rest doesn't deliver big savings and it doesn't provide functionality that helps the business. But we have to do it to comply with Sarbanes Oxley. If we cut it, we're out of compliance with key regulations.

Jorg   Point well taken. So let me qualify my statement and say we cut noncritical projects. The expanding number of regulations has increased our costs, but we can't avoid them. But for those nonessential projects — we shouldn't touch them. What's that old saying, "If it ain't broke, don't fix it"?

Charles   I have the perfect example of what Jorg is talking about. A team that shall remain nameless proposed overhauling a process and group of systems to the tune of $6 million over three years. It made no sense to invest in revamping the process because there were no foreseeable savings or other benefits that would come out of the project.

In fact, I was pretty upset that the business and program managers were wasting the time of our IT staff when the "do nothing" option was the one that made the most business sense. So, moving forward, I expect that each leader in this room will minimize any time wasted planning for initiatives that don't deliver sufficient value.

Kayla   That's a great policy to put into place. Any initiative has to meet the minimum criteria for consideration. Who owns enforcing that policy?

Charles   Carolyn's team owns ensuring that all initiatives meet the minimum criteria before they are presented to executive leadership.

Kayla   Very well. And, speaking of Carolyn, let's talk about the overarching plans that everyone has pulled together. Carolyn, who are the spokespeople from each area?

Carolyn   Cobry will provide the overview of the plan for the business team, Rahul is presenting for engineering and Ben is representing the operations group.

Kayla   Let's start with the business, then engineering, then operations, and finally end with Carolyn presenting the overarching plan and the next steps to take Universal Kingdom from vision to execution.

Cloud Framework - Business

1) Start with mapping 4 key objectives to 3 proposed initiatives

4 - Objectives	3- Proposed Initiatives
1. Increase time to value of key business initiatives impacting competitiveness 2. Transparency for board around profit and loss of technology portfolio 3. Address compliance concerns 4. Cut costs on IT Spend by 30%	1. Rewriting Call Center Application 2. Remote Workforce 3. Private Cloud – with Hybrid hooks

2) Form business teams to work with Product Management to create:
  – Business requirements & benefits (50,000 foot, service levels, and features)
  – Metrics and key performance indicators for success metrics

3) Appoint representatives
  – Map out solution and process requirements for initiatives that meet minimum objectives
  – Run monthly meetings with technology
  – Go to contacts to address any blockers or questions

© 2014, iSpeak Cloud

Cobry   Gladly. Our slide shows how we plan to start with the four objectives that Charles gave us earlier today: increasing time to value, transparency around profit and loss, compliance and cutting IT spend by 30%.

We'll use the objectives and our three initiatives as focal points for mapping meetings. The meetings will center on scoping out requirements and next. We've appointed go-to contacts to help remove any roadblocks that come up. We'll meet monthly to monitor progress and measure key performance indicators for progress toward completing the business case.

Kayla   Who are the three representatives and what areas to they cover?

Cobry   (*Laughing*) Number 3 on our list is to appoint representatives. More than likely it will be more than three. We will appoint one primary representative per area per your suggestion in the workshop.

Kayla   That sounds like a great plan. Rahul, what are your thoughts on the business plan?

Rahul   It seems pretty comprehensive and well thought out. Where will the engineering representation be during the process?

Cobry   Engineering will have one representative, like everyone else. Ideally, we would have an architect with us during planning and throughout the execution cycle. Your team will be critical in helping us determine the costing model.

Ben   I assume you're also including someone from operations engineering as well.

Cobry   Yes. As stated, we'll have one from each area.

Kayla   Rahul, are you ready to provide the overview for engineering?

Cloud Framework - Engineering

1) Form development scrum teams for functional projects/initiatives

> **3- Proposed Initiatives**
>
> 1. Rewriting Call Center Application
> 2. Remote Workforce
> 3. Private Cloud – with Hybrid hooks

2) Assign architects to work in business teams to create technical solutions
   - Create minimum success metrics based on service level agreements, scalability, & continuity
   - Research technical solutions based on requirements
   - Work with Product Management to create Request for Information & Request for Proposals
   - Create short list of solutions to evaluate

3) Pilot Project
   - Create Pilot Project with top 2-3 vendors to evaluate solutions, hidden costs or requirements
   - Finalize plans (resourcing, timing, technical solutions, metrics) with cross functional team
   - Present final to leadership with recommendations
   - Map out solution and process requirements for initiatives that meet minimum objectives

4) Attend meetings for functional groups to review metrics, plans, and roadblocks

Rahul The engineering plan feeds off the business plan, thanks to Carolyn. We'll focus on the primary initiatives because the assumption is that the key business objectives will already have been baked into the BRD and user stories. Note, though, that to achieve the 30 percent reduction in IT expenses, we'll consider using open source in lieu of vendor-specified code or products wherever possible. We'll also evaluate usage and true cost of cloud solutions. Meaning, if we have to create a succinct business continuity strategy with redundancy, we'll need a copy of whatever solutions are in place on premise or with another provider. There's an expense associated with this, particularly with SaaS solutions. In addition, if we need a caching solution to reduce latency due to multiple calls over the Internet, those costs will also have to be calculated.

Jorg Those are interesting points, Rahul. Are you saying that we have to still develop onsite solutions?

Rahul   Not exactly. If the SaaS vendor's site goes down, we still need a way to service our customers. Kayla made a really good point this week. Service providers depend on network and hardware, just like we do in our data center. So they are just as open to the possibility of an outage as we are. We have to plan for business continuity in case their site goes down.

For example, we need some form of redundancy so our agents can still process calls and access the system. A caching solution will help us with that to a point. Hosting our customer database on premise will also help. Otherwise our automatic dialer will no longer work, or our agents won't have the name of the customer they are trying to process. Essentially, they won't be able to assist customers. That's too big a risk to the company.

Cobry   Jorg, business continuity is a necessary evil. But can we write that off? It's in-house development. Or can we negotiate a discount with vendors for the parts we still have to do? How does this work?

Jorg   All good questions, Cobry. We'll have to follow up with fixed asset accounting to see if it's possible to write those pieces off. The accounting guys would have a better idea of what we can and can't do from a tax standpoint. I know if it were an on-premise solution, the answer would be a definite yes. But cloud is tricky. We should be able to have procurement negotiate a discount for items that we cannot use because of our size. Carolyn, can you please follow up with purchasing?

Carolyn   Absolutely. All excellent points.

Kayla   Can anyone tell me what we could do to help the business understand key points needed in their planning?

Marissa   A checklist typically helps us in the call center to track changes.

Elizabeth   Yes, we use them quite a bit in engineering for planning. Didn't think to have them transcend to the business.

Kayla What are some key items we heard about today that need to be on the checklist?

Elizabeth A few of the ones I heard today that need to be done *before* deciding which route to take are:

- A 50,000-foot view of requirements and a BRD

- A full understanding of business continuity requirements and additional development needs

- A review of asset implications with fixed asset accounting before selecting a vendor route for SaaS, cloud or on-premise solution

- A review of what tools or solutions we have in place, as well as impacts such as integrations, network connectivity and load

- Insight into what resource needs would be for a pilot — at a minimum — and how many pilot teams will be needed

Kayla Any other items for our checklist?

Marissa Preliminary training requirements. And also any help that will be needed from the service desk to support the pilots.

Ben I also think we should include an initial idea of where the pilots will be set up — such as production or development. And we should include any special monitoring or considerations to avoid issues in production when we roll out on a large scale.

Andrew I would also include who the pilot users will be. We need an idea of security implications and any changes — things like updating permissions in Active Directory and upgrading hardware for users in the pilot. The business will need to provide at least a ballpark list in terms of how many users we need for a successful pilot, and what are the blackout periods such as the Christmas holiday season.

Kayla   All great ideas. But I think we are getting a little bit beyond what we need for a checklist. For example, Andrew's last points should be covered in the BRD, which is already a checklist item. Ben, are you ready to cover the operations planning summary?

Cloud Framework - Operations

1) Assign Operations and Support representatives to functional projects/initiatives

> **3- Proposed Initiatives**
> 1. Rewriting Call Center Application
> 2. Remote Workforce
> 3. Private Cloud – with Hybrid hooks

2) Assign operations architect to work in business teams to create technical solutions
   - Site network, datacenter, client, and/or other system requirements
   - Review change management for integration, Tuning and Timing with other initiatives and general operations

3) Pilot Project planning and support
   - Participate in pilot planning – help desk, network security, client and server operations teams
   - Procure and/or create environments for deployment, packaging, testing
   - Work with Engineering and Business to create launch plan, key performance metrics and go/no go decision checklist
   - Create Day 1 support model to be tested during pilot and adjusted for large scale rollout
   - Pull CMDB reports for footprint and asset details to determine sizing and footprint requirements

© 2014, iSpeak Cloud

Ben   Carolyn guided us in the same direction as the other two teams. So, as you can see from the slide, we focused on the three primary initiatives with the assumption that the business and product teams were setting up the link between the corporate objectives and initiative focus.

Just as the application requirements will need to be balanced to support the pilot, our operations architect will need to size network, data center, client and other impacts such as telephony switch, client OS and hardware upgrades.

Change management architects or representatives will need to participate to review the impact of other changes in the environment for the pilot, such as major upgrades, other conflicting pilots and utilization of help desk and program management resources.

Finally, we added quite a bit to planning the pilot and feeding in costs for the operational aspects of the pilot. This is an area where my team is severely underfunded. More often than not we are an afterthought. We aren't included in the planning phase. Given that we own the pipes and plumbing, it doesn't make sense to exclude us. We're the only ones who can determine if our pipes can support the demand without increasing costs or complexity.

We've created a checklist for the inception phase and it includes all the things we need to do up front to make the pilot successful. Things like creating test and pilot environments for the operations team, go/no-go decisions for releasing prior to vendor involvement, launch plan, KPIs and what we have to have in place to support the application on Day 1 of the pilot. These last items are critical because often the vendors provide what they think we need or push to release faster to make some quarter milestone. We have to look after our best interests and determine what is needed by when and by whom.

Kayla   Anything else we should add to the operations team's list?

Jorg   Costs of any changes in technology and ensuring that the operations resources working on the initial pilot resources are part of CapEx and can assess true costs of the pilot.

Marissa   Ben, we need to know what areas of the help desk you'll need to tap into for skill sets and expertise.

Carolyn   I like the fact that both teams are tied into the projects and initiatives. We'll need to tie back the costs. This will make collating the data for interdependent costs easier than the typical siloed approach. Also, we should not overlook the compliance and audit perspective. Even if a specific approach is more cost effective, it may not be possible due to negative implications for compliance and audit.

Kayla   Carolyn, would you like to present the overarching plan to pull the teams together from a product and program perspective?

Cloud Framework – Program & Product

1) Coordinate plans across groups around service objectives & initiatives

4 - Objectives	3- Proposed Initiatives
1. Increase time to value of key business initiatives impacting competitiveness 2. Transparency for board around profit and loss of technology portfolio 3. Address compliance concerns 4. Cut costs on IT Spend by 30%	1. Rewriting Call Center Application 2. Remote Workforce 3. Private Cloud – with Hybrid hooks

2) Create, update, and integrate business cases across 3 initiatives to 1 succinct plan

3) Create master plans, BRDs, and adjusted calendar (Integration, Tuning, Timing)

4) Host meetings for functional groups to review metrics, plans, and roadblocks
   - Functional meetings; weekly (review requirements, detailed plans for teams)
   - Cross functional meetings; bi-weekly to monthly (review cross functional interdependencies, roadmap)
   - Leadership review meetings; monthly (review metrics and go/no go)

Carolyn   Sure, but before we get started, I'm curious as to why we didn't cover this section at the beginning?

Kayla   The idea is to plan from bottom up and top down. To ensure everyone has a voice, we had to enable them to speak first. This forces leadership to consider all inputs and actively listen to each perspective. This is particularly important in companies that are organized in silos.

Carolyn   Makes sense. Our piece is last but not least. The program and product teams will work together to coordinate the strategy based on the requirements — and the execution of the plan across the functional teams to minimize confusion and maintain consistency.

Our strategy and planning must consider all aspects of our execution strategy to achieve the primary corporate objectives and top three initiatives needed to support those objectives. The technology needed to support them will roll up under those initiatives under the guidance of engineering.

Our individual teams will be responsible for rolling up all plans into one single business initiative that is calculated based on inputs from accounting, engineering, operations, the business and compliance teams. We will be responsible for tracking metrics and measuring where we are with respect to overall performance. And we'll be course correcting as needed.

Our teams will also be responsible for coordinating the BRDs, master plans and overall integration, tuning and timing across the initiatives. We will have three types of meetings:

- First, our group will participate in the weekly functional meetings to ensure that inputs from each individual group are shared across groups and that each group is on track with plans.

- The second set of meetings will be cross-functional sessions hosted by the lower-level teams every two weeks to update teams on critical success factors and progress, and to address any roadblocks.

- The third type of meetings will bring leadership up to date on our progress each month. Topics will include metrics and overall successes related to our initiatives as well as roadblocks.

ⓘ Charles   This level of transparency will be great. I like the fact that senior leaders will be tuned into the overall program without having to attend every meeting. I'm convinced this will reduce confusion. Is it possible have some metrics via email on a more frequent basis? Once a month seems like a long time.

Elizabeth The program team can distribute weekly status reports in addition to providing critical metrics in the monthly meeting. Will that work?

Charles That would be great. We should publish the high-level schedule on a centralized repository so the entire company can have visibility into progress, changes and overall advantages the solution is delivering or will deliver.

Kayla Great work. Congratulations to all of you. We've completed our job here. I would, however, like to do a quick recap of what we covered over the last three days.

Cloud Framework – Recap

1) Identify key corporate objectives and supporting initiatives

4 - Objectives	3- Proposed Initiatives
1. Increase time to value of key business initiatives impacting competitiveness 2. Transparency for board around profit and loss of technology portfolio 3. Address compliance concerns 4. Cut costs on IT Spend by 30%	1. Rewriting Call Center Application 2. Remote Workforce 3. Private Cloud – with Hybrid hooks

2) Understand challenges and map out routes to Cloud value

3) Appoint representatives and functional groups (Business, Technology, Ops)

4) Map out framework to create and execute on Cloud vision

© 2014, iSpeak Cloud

Kayla First, if you noticed we identified the key objectives from leadership. Elizabeth, can you talk about what we did after Charles established the objectives?

Elizabeth We used the objectives as a guide to set policies and precedence for our overall cloud strategy. We defined who can do what. Then we created a list of initiatives that would support the company's objectives. We prioritized the list based on business benefits. What's exciting to me is that now decisions on what to fund are much easier because they are based on business value.

Kayla   Exactly. Think about the laundry list of items that we started with. It's overwhelming when you're faced with a list like that and you have no insight into the value or implications to the company. And think about how easily you were able to distill that list down to three primary initiatives once you started thinking in terms of business value.

Now that you have a good handle on the company objectives and the primary initiatives, it's time to look back at the challenges to mapping costs back to cloud value. Who wants to recap our discussion on mapping cloud value?

Rahul   The gist of it is more about creating high-level guidelines we can give to employees so they can make the best choices based on a framework that addresses key challenges such as regulatory compliance. For example, if an applications engineer works on regulated applications, he can request a virtual environment on the local system or work with a provider that adheres to our compliance guidelines.

Kayla   Rahul, that does cover the gist of it. Of course, there is a lot more to this section that needs to be considered around challenges. It's important to capture the potential risks and understand challenges not only for the end users per Rahul's examples, but also for internal employees.

Another example that comes to mind is resources. Does Universal Kingdom possess the necessary skill sets? Another challenge is conflicting trends, such as balancing the demand for continuous delivery with the company's ability to absorb frequent change.

Ben   Understanding those challenges is really critical for operations to be able to sustain the solution in production. We can't assign resources and create teams and a support structure if we don't know what skills, resources and solutions we need.

Kayla   Well said, Ben. You started to elaborate on the next step we reviewed, which is assigning resources based on initiatives, challenges and solutions. The key to being successful is to ensure that there is representation across the silos in the cross-functional teams executing on the vision for each initiative. These resources will be the ones primarily executing and updating this group on the progress using clearly defined performance metrics.

Our role is to serve as the coach — to guide and provide a playbook for the teams to execute. Be careful when you're asked to make decisions at this level because it will distract critical resources from making key decisions. For example, after a botched deployment of critical software at a large healthcare system, the CIO decided that that all deployments into production required approval. This mandate lasted two weeks, at which point the CIO realized what a big mistake it was. Why? At his level, he was too far removed to understand the implications of his decisions. The hundreds of weekly deployments turned into a mountain of delays and bottlenecks causing backlash from the business. Even the smallest of changes to the website and smaller applications started to take months to roll out due to the backlog. Here's the bottom line: As leaders, you need to empower the teams you appoint to do their jobs successfully.

Now, back to our slide. Item number four. Executing on the cloud framework. We need to drill down into the five primary principles that the framework is built on. My next slide summarizes those principles.

Kayla   We've already talked about this one quite a bit and in today's exercise you identified the low-hanging fruit and came up with a list of three initiatives. With respect to integrations, keep it small and manageable. No more than three to five.

I worked with a company that started with more than 40 integrations. It was no surprise that the staff couldn't get the cloud pilot or initiatives off the ground. The solution had to be scaled back and broken into manageable chunks. Remember, if you swallow a whale whole, you'll choke on it. But if you cut it up and make sushi, you will delight not only yourself but those around you.

Charles   Kayla, we all love sushi. But I don't want to talk about food. I want to say a few words about item number 2. I expect every leader in this room to be a gate keeper. I don't want any services or projects kicked off without a clear way to manage success. And by success, I'm talking about making a contribution to the company's bottom line.

$Jorg   I agree. So we have to leverage not only the simple cash flow model but also profit and loss models to determine the best possible outcomes for the business. We need to evaluate everything to ensure the juice is worth the squeeze. In other words, the business case should help drive what routes are available to a given project. We have to make sure that no future investments are made without proof that they will yield results that are at least tenfold — every dollar spent should result in 10 dollars coming back.

Kayla   Sound words and a good mantra to live by. We are really close to wrapping up, so I will be brief with the last two points. Once you have identified your

> Start small, with a handful of services. Then expand as processes, skill sets and solutions mature.

priorities it's important to pilot the cloud initiative. In short, don't start with a big bang approach. Start with a handful of services and expand out as the overall processes, skill sets and solutions mature. It's the crawl-walk-run mantra. And going from walk to run typically has to happen pretty fast. So an important purpose of the pilot is gaining an understanding of what it will take to expand the solution on an enterprise scale.

Another favorite piece of advice I have received is to architect for change and for a hybrid solution. Even if your initial project is around private cloud, take into

> Architect for change and consider how you might expand to a hybrid cloud environment in the future.

account how you might expand it to address a hybrid environment. As part of your pilot of policies, remember that it's much easier to turn around a race car than a ship. The bigger the launch the bigger the risk of damage or confusion — especially if things are constantly changing. You have to market your cloud efforts to your employees and colleagues for them to truly understand the value.

My last takeaway is ensuring you measure results or effectiveness of the solution on a regular basis. And use those metrics to help you constantly enhance your cloud strategy.

So, our workshop is done. I want to thank each one of you for your participation and hard work. You have the framework and a solid action plan to move forward. Now your success or failure in cloud rests in your own hands.

ⓘ Charles   Kayla, thank you. We have really enjoyed the last few days and I feel like we've all learned a lot and accomplished a lot. And I just want to remind all of you on this team that we have a responsibility to not only execute but also enforce the rules of engagement within our respective teams. I'm counting on each of you to make our cloud vision a reality. As a follow up to this workshop, I'm asking each of you to be prepared to discuss your execution strategy to the plans we created in next week's staff meeting.

Food For Thought

Action	Considerations
Who would you invite to the table?	Have you invited the appropriate combination of decision makers and implementers to identify critical steps and make key decisions to create a cohesive plan? Is there representation across business and IT? If not, why not? What do you need to do to change that? Have you clearly defined their roles and objectives for this initiative?
Create your own BRD	Create your own BRD. Remember, start small and get the experience of mapping a smaller cloud initiative such as the implementation of a SaaS Solution. Do you have enough information? Too much? Are you able to gather what you need from those you would invite to your table? Why or why not?
Revisit the profit-and-loss exercise	Try to create your own mini-P&L exercise to determine if the juice is worth the squeeze from your BRD. Start by ranking your business requirements based on value to the company (intrinsic and monetary) from the business requirements documents. Input or pull resources and velocity to meet service levels. Input what you think will be both your capital and operational expenses. Remember to keep this first pass small — a few solutions, a few resources. This is just an exercise. How would you apply this to your cloud execution strategy? What factors will play the biggest role in selecting the right initiatives to invest in? What factors often play into it that shouldn't? Do your current initiatives align with the overall company strategy? If not, what will you need to achieve alignment?

Bibliography

Tech Target, "Cloud Washing," 2011,
http://searchcloudstorage.techtarget.com/definition/cloud-washing

[1] Mitchel Smith, David, "Hype Cycle for Cloud Computing 2013", Gartner, Inc. 2013

Heekal, Rheem, "What is a Cash Flow Statement", 2010, Investopedia,
http://www.investopedia.com/articles/04/033104.asp

2010, Definition of Capital Expenditure,
http://www.investopedia.com/terms/c/capitalexpenditure.asp

"Agile Software Development" Wikipedia, 2014,
http://en.wikipedia.org/wiki/Agile_software_development

"Definition of Profit and Loss; P&L", Investopedia, 2014,
http://www.investopedia.com/terms/p/plstatement.asp

"Service-level agreement", Wikipedia, 2014, http://en.wikipedia.org/wiki/Service-level_agreement

"Operating Expenses", Investopedia, 2014,
http://www.investopedia.com/terms/o/operating_expense.asp

"Depreciation", Investopedia, 2014,
http://www.investopedia.com/terms/d/depreciation.asp

Reh, John, "Key Performance Indicators (KPI): How an organization defines and measures progress toward its goals", About.com, 2014, http://management.about.com/cs/generalmanagement/a/keyperfindic_2.htm

"Virtual Private Cloud", Wikipedia, 2014,
http://en.wikipedia.org/wiki/Virtual_Private_Cloud

Glossary

Term	Definition
Agile Development Model	A group of software development methods based on iterative and incremental development, in which requirements and solutions evolve through collaboration between self-organizing, cross-functional teams. It promotes adaptive planning, evolutionary development and delivery, a time-boxed iterative approach, and encourages rapid and flexible response to change. It is a conceptual framework that promotes foreseen tight iterations throughout the development cycle.
Application virtualization	Software technology that improves portability, manageability and compatibility of applications by encapsulating them from the underlying operating system on which they are executed.
Business Requirements Document (BRD)	Document that contains the primary constructs of the requirements for a given IT service. A BRD should include the overall framework for defining minimum requirements for reliability, availability, serviceability, supportability, scalability and security.
Business Service Management (BSM)	Unification of people, processes and technology across service delivery, service support and service management to proactively address needs of the business.
CapEx	Short for capital expense. Capital

expenses are funds used by a company to acquire or upgrade physical assets such as property, industrial buildings or equipment. This type of outlay is made by companies to maintain or increase the scope of their operations. These expenditures can range from repairing a roof to building a brand new factory. They can be depreciated over the life of the benefit.

Cash Flow Statement
Financial statements that do not include the amount of future incoming and outgoing cash that has been recorded on credit or benefits such as depreciation benefits. Cash flow statements look at three distinct areas in which cash enters and leaves the company: financing, investing and operations.

Cloud Bursting
The lifting and shifting of an application or service that is typically run in a data center or private cloud to a public or virtual private cloud entity to address requirements for additional capacity or demand.

Cloud Calibration
Synchronization and creation of policies and procedures that govern the use of the various types of clouds by an organization. This includes but is not limited to policies across organizational units or cloud providers, or cloud bursting or use of different types of clouds based on role.

Cloud Framework
Process framework that integrates a cohesive strategy across multidisciplined

groups including but not limited to engineering, business, operations, audit, governance, finance, architecture and product management. All components of the framework are tied together through checks and balances across the various teams to determine best strategy and policy around their use and implementation of cloud computing.

Cloud Washing	The purposeful or deceptive trend of a vendor to rebrand an old product or service by attaching the word *cloud* to it.
Consumerization of IT	Trend in which new technology emerges first in the consumer market and then spreads to businesses, resulting in the convergence of the IT and consumer electronics industries, and a shift in IT innovation from large businesses to the home.
Depreciation	A method of allocating the cost of a tangible asset over its useful life. Businesses depreciate long-term assets for both tax and accounting purposes.
DevOps	Integrates disciplines of software development and IT operations to create a cohesive, collaborative, integrated process for iterative development and delivery of applications in a more secure, predictive and time-efficient manner. DevOps targets quality assurance, delivery, and development teams and processes.
Digital Native	Person born during or after the introduction of digital technology and who has gained familiarity with digital

concepts as a result of interacting with technology from an early age.

End-of-Life Benefits	Monetary and soft benefits derived from decommissioning older software or hardware that is no longer in use or not used enough to justify the cost to run it.
Hybrid Cloud	An integrated infrastructure environment that leverages both on-premise (private cloud) and off-premise providers to address capacity requirements for applications (either SaaS or Computer-off-the-Shelf).
Infrastructure as a Service (IaaS)	Software technology, also known as cloud infrastructure services, that delivers computer infrastructure. Typically a platform virtualization environment that includes raw (block) storage and networking as a service.
Integration, Tuning and Timing (ITT)	Framework for determining best path forward for integrating multiple workstreams in a complex implementation such as a multilayered cloud strategy based on number of integrations, amount of tuning and anticipated time period.
Key Performance Indicators (KPIs)	Quantifiable measurements, agreed to beforehand, that reflect the critical success factors of an organization. They differ depending on the organization.
Licensing as a Service	A service offering that tracks, updates and reports on software/hardware license usage versus what was purchased. The service will enable customers to

distinguish between internal purchased and external cloud solutions to reduce double charging customers.

Massively Multi-Player Online/Role Playing Game (MMORPG)	Genre of role-playing video games in which a very large number of players interact with each other in a virtual game world.
Master Planning Spreadsheet	Cohesive planning spreadsheet or tool that pulls together resources, requirements, timeframes and applications needed for a given service.
Net Present Value (NPV)	The difference between the present value of cash inflows and the present value of cash outflows. NPV is used in capital budgeting to analyze the profitability of an investment or project.
Nonpersistent Virtual Machine	Virtual machine that, based on user click, is either assembled on demand from a golden image or cloned on demand with appropriate applications layered.
OpEx	Short for operating expenses. A category of expenditures that a business incurs as a result of performing its normal business operations. In IT, for example, this would include what is required to keep the business running, such as network, internet and email.
Platform as a Service (PaaS)	Delivery of a computing platform and solution stack as a service. PaaS offerings facilitate deployment of applications without the cost and complexity of buying and managing the underlying hardware, software and provisioning hosting

capabilities. It provides all facilities required to support the complete lifecycle of building and delivering web applications and services that are made available on the Internet.

Persistent Virtual Machine	Preconfigured, set virtual machine image with applications and configurations preinstalled and available for user access.
Private Cloud	Computing environment (also called on-premise cloud) in which infrastructure is operated for a single organization. It can be managed and/or hosted either internally or by a third party.
Product Manager (Service)	Individual responsible for defining, refining and ensuring that the overall stability, health and anticipated profit and loss benefits are obtained from a given service offering.
Profit and Loss Statement (P&L)	A financial statement that summarizes the revenues, costs and expenses incurred during a specific period of time, usually a fiscal quarter or year. These records provide information that shows the ability of a company to generate profit by increasing revenue and reducing costs. The P&L statement is also known as a statement of profit and loss, an income statement or an income and expense statement.
Public Cloud	Collection of external cloud computing resources (also called off-premise cloud) that are dynamically provisioned by offsite third-party providers to the general public on a self-service basis over the

	Internet via web applications/web services.
Quasi-private Cloud	Dedicated set of private cloud resources that is sectioned off in a public cloud provider facility but managed by a private cloud administrator.
Software as a Service (SaaS)	Software delivery model in which software and its associated data are hosted centrally (typically in the cloud) and accessed over the Internet, usually from a thin client with a web browser.
Service Level Agreements (SLA)	Part of a service contract in which a service is formally defined. The term SLA is sometimes used to refer to the contracted delivery time of the service or performance.
Time to Value (TTV)	The amount of time required to reach initial goals of either savings or increased revenue. Anticipated time to value is often used to create the business case for a given service or project.
Universal Clients	Applications and data that follow the user across multiple devices, networks and data stores in a secure and reliable manner.
Virtual Private Cloud (VPC)	An on-demand configurable pool of shared computing resources allocated within a public cloud environment, providing a certain level of separation between the different organizations using the resources.

Appendix A — Business Requirements Document Template

Many believe that a BRD is "waterfall development" but that only leads them to fall short in understanding the framework or essential constructs that need to be in place. Agile does not mean not understanding or knowing the basics of what you are trying to build. Think of the Agile BRD like the "blueprint" for a house. It provides key information needed to frame the solution that you are trying to provide so that you build a solid foundation. Non-essential information like color of paint on the walls, carpet or tile, or type of cabinets is not selected until later and not typically included in the blueprint. In this construct the Agile BRD serves the same purpose. It provides enough information so that key decisions can be made, a solid architecture can be put in place and a strong business case created.

What are the essential components of an Agile BRD?

- **Short and consise**. Unlike Waterfall – the Agile BRD should be no more than 20-25 pages on average.
- **Problem and Solution** should be clearly defined in general constructs.
- **Target Audience** personas and general requirements for the users and executive business leadership.
- **Ramp Requirements** of end users over what period of time should be well known. In other words understand the business plan for rollout and ramping new users to the system.
- **Key Stakeholders** assigned and bought in from business and technology.
- **Objectives** of the proposed solution and how it will resolve problem.
- **Key Performance Indicators** to test whether the solution is on track to solve the problem or needs to be adjusted
- **High Level Requirements and Volume Forecasting** to frame the solution and understand forecasting to make key decisions around cloud – private, public, hybrid
- **Reliability** should define how reliable or the actual up time of the system
- **Availability** should define when the application or service needs to be available to the users per the service level agreement
- **Serviceability** should define peak from non-peak times and when IT can make major versus minor changes to the system without impacting business
- **Scalability** should define how many users are anticipated on the system during a peak load.

- **Supportability** should define the type and level of service/support the end users will expect. For example, knowledgebase, chat, online help, and/or call center.
- **Security** should define regulations and security measures need to be in place given the nature of the service being provided. For example, a health care service may require extra constructs for the Health Insurance Portability Accountabilty Act.
- **Task analysis** that are typically created by the Program Management Office should be attached to reduce back and forth and so development understands what other things the user has to do to complete the tasks such as use other applications, physical constructs, etc.
- **Systems and Precedence** – a high level list of targeted systems to integrate to and what their priority will be based on either savings to the company or criticality for ease of use.

Effective BRDs will be created with the business for business facing services and with the solutions product manager for cross application requirements. In other words the services will intersect in the cloud. If you do not understand the basic framework for the service you will not have a good handle on costs, what the key cloud strategy needs to be for that application, or how to truly meet the needs of the business.

The BRD should be a living document that records the requirements of collaboration and changes that occur along the way from a high level. What it will provide is a solid framework similar to a blueprint to enable both business and technology to come together prepared to discuss basic constructs without being bogged down in the details.

Looking for a good Business Requirements Template? Go to www.ispeakcloud.com to request a copy of the template used for the book and workshops.

Appendix B — Master Planning Worksheet

The Master Planning Worksheet is the glue that enables the service manager to tie together all the critical pieces across the solutions to determine best path forward, update budgets, understand resource constraints, and coordinate swim lanes across services. The Master Planning Worksheet would be best served as an application that is created to integrate the various inputs from both manual and existing systems to allow Product Management, Program Management, and Executive Leadership visibility into the current state of the solution.

There are cases where this is not possible due to either resource or time constraints – then it is possible to leverage Microsoft Excel or Microsoft Access with macros or functions as a stop gap solution. The key is to include the essential components that need to be tracked. Those essential components are:

- **Summary** of high level requirements (50,000 foot level), anticipated versus actual release, what the interdependencies include per service/requirement, what cross functional areas will be impacted (to identify hot spots), and what products can be end of life when the service is rolled out
- **Resources** broken down between capitalizable (developers, quality assurance, architects, database engineers) and non-capitablizable (management and administrative). Listed by name and function along with average velocity hourly (not by user stories or points as they vary)
- **Requirements** (also known as Epics) at a 10,000-20,0000 foot level that link back to the higher level service and are listed in order of priority and impact (higher savings higer rank) to product Agile Burn Down per release. These should be done at least 1 release prior. Detailed user stories will be linked back to these Epics in whatever the Agile tool that is used by the team such as Jira. Those that do not make the current revision are moved to the next Agile release cycle until the burn down is complete or project is terminated.
- **Mapping** of swim lanes across resources and timelines to have a high level visibility of hot spots, cold spots and run forecasting for adjustments.
- **Timeline** that calculates maximum number of sprints within a targeted release date, number of targeted releases – major and minor, and blackout periods for release such as Holiday Season for an Online Retailer.
- **Forecasting tab** provides a duplicate of the summary page but enables Leadership to adjust either releases, resources, or timelines to calculate potential impact of changes that may be needed due to other higher priority items coming up

- **Budget burndown** – breakdown of budget consumed for both OpEx and CapEx pulled from resource planning tools and asset management system. This tab would integrate to/export to a profit and loss statement for IT spening/costs with any timeline adjustments including burn down, depreciation schedule, and impact on contract budgets.

Looking for a good Master Planning Templates? Go to www.ispeakcloud.com to request a copy of the template used for the book and workshops.

Appendix C — DevOps

About DevOps by Paul Pessner

Since 2009, the term DevOps has been associated with an innovative and cross-discipline effort to improve software team communications, process flows and collaborations across software application development (Dev) teams and IT operations and production (Ops) teams. For many reasons the Dev and Ops teams became increasingly isolated from each other with growing process inefficiencies, fragility and complexities. The Dev and Ops functions evolved into highly specialized roles and tasks within siloed and segmented teams. The large project team sizes, scope and estimated timelines were further challenged by:

- Complex software environments that encompass layers of many generations of technical debt
- Isolated conversations and decision-making in specialized silos with limited knowledge
- Little incentive to involve or collaborate with upstream or downstream stakeholders
- Minimal accountability for unnecessary delays, cost overages or business disruptions
- Reward systems for partial contributions with limited connections to business success metrics

DevOps emphasizes the need for improved communication, collaboration and integrations across the organization to improve software quality and agility.

A number of interesting enablers have contributed to the DevOps efforts:

- DevOps aligns well with agile development with the smaller teams and scope, and faster cycles.
- DevOps advocates more generalized (cross-discipline) software engineering skills and expertise.
- DevOps encourages a collaborative culture of innovative exploration and experimentation.
- DevOps promotes "process ownership" to smooth transitions and accelerate fast-fix efforts.

- DevOps can be cost effective and predictable for businesses needing more software agility.

DevOps has proven to be a successful model in both large and small organizations. It addresses many of the delays and disruptions associated with slow-moving, big-bang projects and partial contributions by specialized contributors with rewards systems disassociated from the business vision, goal or need.

The Dev in DevOps — that is, the software application development teams focused on the preproduction project phases — often advocates agile (Scrum) development and *continuous integration* (CI). CI accelerates the frequency of the developers' integration efforts (early and often) and includes more automation for build and test functions, such as unit test, functional test and performance tests, to improve code quality. For many Dev teams this has facilitated the blending of development- and QA-siloed roles and has sped up the project cycles while improving software quality.

The Ops in DevOps — that is, the IT operations and production teams focused on managing the software services for the business or BSM — often advocates agile (Kanban) for development and engineering teams, and *continuous delivery* (CD). CD extends CI practices, ensuring that the Dev software is ready to deploy, and accelerates the deployment processes by leveraging cross-discipline collaboration and transparency with innovative automation technologies.

Today, the applications are often much smaller (team size and project scope) with less risk of widespread disruptions. By leveraging the fast-track CI and CD automation designs with a DevOps model, new applications can accelerate their introductions to the business in the most efficient and cost-effective way. Increasingly, organizations are finding the predictability of their DevOps teams and the quality of their software to be a strategic differentiator in shaping software-driven business agility strategies.

Most DevOps conversations break into one of three categories:

1. Dev-driven DevOps — Business-driven software development
2. Ops-driven DevOps — Performance-driven software sustainability
3. Business-driven DevOps — Software-driven business agility

Dev-driven DevOps: Many Dev-driven DevOps conversations tend to speak about agile and DevOps interchangeably. The agile concepts, principles and practices in the Dev world quickly run into challenges with status quo IT practices and the processes in the Ops world. Legacy Ops policies — for example, ITIL and CMMI — are designed to control change and block the smaller apps, running on faster release cycles. The Dev teams quickly discover the need to collaborate with the Ops teams, especially change managers and systems administrators, to get their apps deployed in a timely manner. In this context, DevOps is simply seen as:

> *An agile "self-organizing" effort with software engineers (Dev and Ops)*
> *solving an (internal) software delivery problem in response to the demands of*
> *the business.*

This type of DevOps effort is a "business-driven software development" effort that grows the number of collaborating (in-house) team members as the agile practices gain velocity. These teams see little need for nonsoftware contributors to get involved. They often resist the idea of changing structures, policies and processes, initially preferring to work around the legacy structures (smuggling in innovation). These Dev-driven DevOps conversations often fail to address long-term business costs, resolve bigger systemwide organizational issues, fully understand the impact on support teams or provide "at scale" change strategies.

Ops-driven DevOps: Many Ops-driven DevOps conversations tend to include Kanban, IT modernization, cloud/virtualization and new technology frameworks such as Chef, Puppet, CF Engine and ARA in their DevOps conversations. DevOps in this context is a borderless IT conversation. Ops engineers have expanded their roles and discuss concepts such as "Software defined... Data Centers, Storage and Networks" and "Infrastructure as Code." The transparency and flexibility in this new environment reduces the need for much of the manual practices and labor-intensive repetitive activities. This type of Ops-driven DevOps conversation evolves with performance-driven software sustainability concerns with a high sensitivity around quality and stability. The Ops team likes to have policy-driven automation guidelines (engineering in the innovation) and typically requests more standards and discipline by agile Dev teams.

Business-driven DevOps: Many business-driven DevOps conversations are hyperaware of the changing markets, the need for competitive differentiation and new technology. These conversations tend to focus on time to market and hiring new teams for a new pilot with little regard for existing resources, standards or long-term costs. In general, this type of business-driven DevOps conversation will see software-driven business agility as a net new investment (buying new team innovation) and often underutilizes the pre-existing teams and shared resources.

This book addresses many of the conversations that are "bigger" than the DevOps agenda. And while DevOps is finding traction at a global level, many of the business conversations still need to be factored into DevOps efforts.

Made in the USA
San Bernardino, CA
18 April 2016